Early Praise For Tom Spear and Carry On!

Cliff Chadderton, President of War Amps Society

"(Tom Spear) has been a constant inspiration to me . . . His take on life is simple, direct and should be communicated to every adult and child in this country . . . This book will serve as a beacon to all Canadians."

Susan Papp, TV producer

"Tom Spear is a living testimonial to the strength of the human spirit. Meeting him is inspirational. He's full of life experience and although he's had his share of hardships and tragedies, he's still full of enthusiasm and energy. Many of my forty-something friends could learn from him. This book will be a wonderful guiding light to those who are dispirited, hopeless and searching for meaning in life. Tom Spear teaches us that hope in life comes from within, and although it must be nurtured, it will give you great strength in life."

Charlie Mertra, Calgary Seniors Club past president

"Tom Spear is an amazing man. This book will let seniors know what is in store for them if they keep active in many phases of their own personal doings."

Dr. Manfred Hackemann, M.D.

"Tom Spear is amazing. After more than 25 years of being my patient, he still inspires me with his vitality and sheer zest for life. This man does not need a doctor. He needs a coach."

Bill Gillott, Rotarian

"Tom Spear is an inspiration to young and old. About the time I was starting my career, Tom was retiring at age 65. His continuous positive approach to life and boundless energy often provided me with a mental lift. Today I am now retired and Tom is still an inspiration."

Vince Thormin, retired minister

"Tom Spear is an amazing man. He can well be described by Plato, also called Aristocles, the Greek philosopher . . . 'If a man is moderate and contented, then even age is no burden; if he is not, then even youth is evil of cares' . . . This book may awaken readers to the reality of life."

Garth Mann, homebuilder

"Tom Spear is not an old man! Growing up next door to his daughter and son-in-law, I have admired Tom Spear for close to 40 years. Besides inheriting his great genes, his happy demeanor and enjoyment of life and people have contributed to his fulfillment and longevity. This book will create reader interest in the real values of life that often are lost in the fast-paced treadmill we all expose ourselves to."

Bert May, retired train engineman

"Tom Spear is a man of incredible energy. I have known him for a quarter of a century. I first got to know Tom through our mutual interest in sports. In 1975, I started curling in the same league as did Tom and since that time have become a close friend. We golf together and both are active members of Southwood Seniors Club, where Tom is an honorary lifetime member. Over the years, I have come to respect and appreciate Tom's zest for living, wisdom, integrity, family values and commitment to life."

Marj Kirkham, friend

"Tom Spear is a man of integrity, honesty enthusiasm, vitality and continues to grow in wisdom at the age of 102 years. This book is remarkable . . . inspiring . . . a story of one man's ability to live life in abundance for 102 years . . . A must for young and old."

Robert L. Costigan, friend

"He has a great positive outlook and inspires many people with his dynamic personality. This book will (demonstrate) his benefit from a clean and healthy life and that alone is an inspiration for many a younger person. His golf has set an example for all golfers his junior . . . (It) has been a joy for me to know such a phenomenal man."

Foreword

Sometimes, you've just gotta believe.

When I approached Tom Spear about writing this book, I was convinced readers could benefit from his life story, positive attitude, and sheer zest for life. I felt this book would appeal to countless baby boomers as they travel along the road he has already travelled and become seniors. Unfortunately, some influential people didn't share my views. Several publishers rejected proposals to publish this book. Why? Our research has shown that Carry On — the story of a centenarian by a centenarian — is among the first of its kind in Canada. In my opinion, these publishers were simply afraid to take a chance.

In 1998, Tom Spear, his family, and I realized that, if we wanted to publish this book anytime soon, we would have to do it ourselves. Tom, his daughter Dorothy, son-in-law Ron Pike, and I created our own publishing company, Falcon Press, and spent months arranging the printing, promotion and distribution of this publication.

We faced a difficult challenge: Number one, we were all rookies at book publishing and, for simple financial reasons, my duties at the Calgary Herald had to come first. Tom also had commitments in France, Ottawa and Boston while he and his family faced the untimely deaths of two or their loved ones — Tom's granddaughter Laurie Wood and his son-in-law Shig Aoyagi, both of Los Altos, California — and other commitments. Despite these challenges, we never doubted that we would (ahem) carry on. As Tom says, "You have to believe it to achieve it." And we did.

I would like to thank Tom, Ron and Dorothy Pike, Tom's daughter Joyce Aayogi, and the rest of their family for their strong support of my efforts. Their help, co-operation and sheer enthusiasm were invaluable.

I'm also grateful to many others. Johanna Bates, a literary agent and author, provided vital legal services and essential advice whenever

iv

needed. Marianne Helm, an outstanding photographer with whom I have the privilege of working at the Calgary Herald, shot the excellent photos which grace both the front and back of this book. She also went out of her way to arrange a photography studio. Renee Coulman, an exceptionally talented graphic artist, designed the entire cover and patiently put up with my requests for changes. (Thanks also to my old friend Karin Brown for suggesting that Renee design the cover.) Bonnie Monteith was the driving force behind the book's marketing efforts. She completed vital research, devised strategies, prepared promotional materials, arranged Tom Spear's public appearances, and helped set up a distribution program. Tom Seto, a computer expert based at the University of Calgary, spent many hours designing and upgrading our website (www.tomspear.com) and helped prepare the book for printing. Terry Cochrane, an excellent friend, printed rough drafts of chapters and ran errands for me when he probably would have preferred to do something else.

I'm also grateful to several current and former Calgary Herald employees who contributed in many ways: David Bly and Duane Beazer edited the copy and set up the pages for publication; photographers Dean Bicknell, Dave Olecko, David Lazarowych and Mike Sturk supplied and/or reproduced photos which appear in these pages, while Photo Editor Peter Brosseau granted access to the Herald's archives; Shannon Duncan assisted in placing photos in computer files; Bruce Full and Quentin Collier produced the Falcon Press logo; Andy Marshall, an extremely unselfish person, alerted me to Tom Spear's exceptional qualities; the legendary Rick Mofina, the only other guy I know who has appeared on Donahue, showed what it takes to be a dedicated writer; Chris Dawson, John Gradon, David Climenhaga and Ken McGoogan offered insights into the publishing world; Lesley Walsh graciously helped advertise the book; and Don Campbell gave me time off when I needed it. Thanks also for help at other times to: Eric Duhatschek, Larry Wood, Mike Reimer, Ken Hull, Helen Dolik, Juliet Williams, Fred (Gus) Collins, Brock Ketcham; Gyle Konotopetz, Tom

Keyser, Jim MacDonald, Jeff Adams, Sasha Nagy, Lori Ewing, Larry Stevens, Bruce Masterman, Sheldon Alberts, Don Martin, Susan Mate, Ian McKinnon, Eva Ferguson, Monica Zurowski, Joan Crockatt, Crosbie Cotton, Ken King, Glen Miller, Lance Kjersteen, Al Boras, Roman Cooney, Jim Zang, David Heyman and George Bilych, who displayed his wisdom by hiring me. There are too many others to mention but they are also greatly appreciated.

Many thanks also to my old friends from the Grande Prairie Daily Herald- Tribune — especially Bill Scott, Don Moon and Terry McHale — and the Prince Rupert Daily News (i.e. Iain Lawrence). Tom Spear has also helped me see the importance of friends. I am fortunate to have many, outside of work circles, who deserve recognition for helping with this book or just being themselves. Lindsay Gorrill and I have been friends forever. He and his wife Martine (Bertrand) provided a lifetime highlight when they allowed me to be the best man at their wedding, May 26, 1989. I'd say more good things about Lindsay, but his ego is big enough — and I'd probably run out of space. Willie, Anne, Laurie, Larry and Lonnie Gorrill are also great friends. Alex and Sheryl Kwai and their wonderful kids Richard, Katrina and Karyn, make me feel special every time I see them. Their friendship is also a highlight of my life. Other great friends, along with their families, include: Doug (and wife Pin), Elaine, and Michelle Thompson; Dino and Rachel Falcone; Marvin Henry; David Howell, Quinn Howell-Brown and Jill Howell; Bruce and Laura Kagetsu; Mario and Heather Volpe; Mark Noda; Frank Arva; Eion Wotherspoon; Sherry Everett-Vance and Earl Vance; Joyce and Hugh Tait; Ernie and Diane Dickson; Mike and Donna Marino; Jerry and Francine Boyd; Gord and Francesca Ellis; Mike Klassen and Stacey Fruin; Ron and Anita Watson; Benoit St. Amour and Maryse Jobin; Bill Seymour and Helene Ferguson; Doug and Marion Collie; Phil and Darlene Girard; Gary (Suitcase) Smith; Arlene Hill; Sandra Dixon; God (a.k.a. Frank) Devito; Tony T.; Drew Morritt; Dan Roberts; Mike Toth; Gary and Dixie Bain; Richard, Rita and Sylvia Lee; Andrea Roepke; Ron and

Eva Wright; Merv Agar; Dave Leskiw; Colin Sloan; Lorraine Thomas; Gabriella V. Oliver; Doug and Tim Hansen; Demos, Kris and Mark Bata; Tom Brown; and even Samson Chang. Many of the aforementioned and I became friends at Killarney Secondary School in Vancouver, where Roger Flewelling and Lily Genis helped develop my writing skills; Chuck Joy taught me (by example) how to listen, and Ken MacKenzie showed me the value of history.

Tom Spear has also shown me the benefits of a close family and loving relatives. I'm fortunate to have a wonderful mother, Doris Stewart, and brother, Daryl Stewart. They help and inspire me in too many ways to mention — but are always appreciated. George and Marge Jack and Ron and Marianne Davis are like family. It would take several more pages to list all of my relatives. Among the most noteworthy: R.L. Jeffers (whose vision extends way beyond his eyes); Mark, Ryan and Christine Jeffers; Larry, Yvonne, Leah, Noah, Adam and Sheila Jeffers; Todd Jeffers; Judi, Heather, and Jodi-Lyn Newnham and Jamie Boyd; Keith and the rest of the Falconars; Gail Bayne; the Millekers; and David Stewart.

Without the support of all of these people, I could not have believed in this book.

— Monte Stewart

Acknowledgements

It is a pleasure to acknowledge those who have inspired, motivated and strengthened my resolve to record my one hundred and two years of excellent health and happiness. My daughters Joyce and Dorothy and their husbands Shig and Ron have given many hours in collecting pictures and material to produce a smooth running story of rural and city life in which they were personally involved. They were an integral part of my story.

As the years advance and my activities as a senior citizen find favour and admiration, I must thank my sporting and social clubs for their tremendous interest in the achievements a senior citizen can attain: Southwood Seniors, Turner Valley Golf and Country Club, Calgary Seniors Curling Club, Rotary International, the Lions Club, Canadian Pacific Railway employees, Scarboro United Church, Royal Canadian Legion and many close and personal friends who are too numerous to mention but still deeply appreciated. My service in the armed forces in both world wars drew attention as the eightieth anniversary of the Battle of Vimy Ridge arrived in April of 1997. The Department of Veterans Affairs honoured me with an invitation to participate in remembrance services in France and Belgium and again in November of 1997 at the Citizens' Day commemorative service in the House of Commons and Armistice Day, also in Ottawa. In November of 1988, I participated in the eightieth anniversary of the Armistice in France.

An article in the Calgary Herald drew invitations to appear on the CBS Late Late Show with Tom Snyder in Hollywood and Phil Donahue's former syndicated show in New York City. Renewing my driver's license until I'm one hundred and three also sparked special attention. From these exciting events, Monte Stewart, a staff writer with the Calgary Herald, and I have produced this autobiography.

To my neighbours Bruce and Matil Spies, Bert May and his friend

ACKNOWLEDGEMENTS

Patricia, many thanks for taking care of my home while I was on world tours. I would also like to honour my late father, Rev. David Spear and mother Margaret Spear. Their missionary efforts in Innisfail (1893-1900), which was then part of the North West Territory but is now in Alberta, and Manitoba (1900-1946) served as the foundation of our family's honour, love, integrity, and patriotism, which continue today and forever.

I would be remiss if I neglected to record an ideal seventy and a half years with my late wife Margaret. Her inspiration, devotion and total dedication to me and our family are monumental sources of pride and appreciation. She is gone from our home but never from our hearts.

And to Monte Stewart, dear friend, thank you for many hours of warm and intimate friendship.

— Tom Spear

Carry On

This book is dedicated to my loving wife of seventy and a half years, Margaret, also my father and mother, Rev. David and Margaret Spear, my grandson David Pike and my granddaughter Laurie Worthington Wood, all of whom inspired me with great love of home and family.
- Tom Spear

In loving memory of my father, John Alexander (Scoop) Stewart, 1917-1995.
- Monte Stewart

1

The Big Climb

It's November 9, 1998, and I am on a mission. I am climbing — seventy- nine steps, non-stop — to the top of the monument at Bourlon Wood, France. It's a cold, blustery day and the wind presses against my overcoat, but there is no place else I'd rather be. Little do I know that a doctor is following me, just in case I suffer a heart attack, or collapse.

Canada's Veterans Affairs Minister Fred Mifflin, other dignitaries, soldiers and journalists climb with me. When I reach the top of these stairs, I will lay a wreath and salute the many Canadians who laid down their lives here in the name of freedom in World War I.

As I climb, I say a silent prayer: "If I make this, I'll be grateful indeed."

Bourlon Wood was part of the Allies' so called Big Push during the last one hundred days of World War I in 1918. I was here then, as a young man, too. Until today, however, I have never been back. In fact, this is only my second trip to France in the past eighty-two years. I have come back, with seventeen other veterans of World War I still healthy enough to travel overseas, as a guest of the Canadian and French governments.

We are on a ten-day pilgrimage to celebrate the eightieth anniversary of the armistice, now known as Remembrance Day in Canada and Veterans' Day in the United States. Climbing these steps takes a supreme effort. I am one of few World War I veterans still healthy enough to travel overseas, let alone make this climb. Most of our group

1

of seventeen veterans are in wheelchairs or have difficulty walking, but I need no cane or other assistance.

I have also buried my war experiences in the deepest crevasses of my mind for most of the past eighty years. This pilgrimage has revisited places where I actually served in the last one hundred days of the so-called War to End All Wars — such as Mons, Valenciennes and Amiens — and the memories have come rushing back. Images have just broken out. So many things that I had forgotten have come back to life. It feels like my whole being is back in the war.

As I continue to trudge up the stairs, I feel the loss of my older brother Will. As you'll discover in a later chapter, we had left our prairie home together and visited with each other in bunkers on the battlefield. Each one of us would have given his life for the other. Just as I never made it back to Europe, he never returned to Canada. He was fatally wounded near here, at Arras, on September 27, 1918 — only six weeks before the armistice was signed. He was twenty-three. His death continues to have a profound impact on my life today.

Even after all these years, I still feel sorrow from his absence. I had never seen his grave until 1997. How close we came to going home together. I'm also thinking about other soldiers, many from my hometown, who weren't fortunate enough to return. They are very much in my mind as I continue upwards. I recall the motto that I served under with the Royal Canadian Air Force in the Second World War: "Through adversity to the Stars." That was another war, at another time, and I served on home soil, but how appropriate the saying is here today.

As I reach the top of the stairs, I feel it is a real tribute to Will, that I could climb these steps and place a wreath on the cenotaph that represented a victory. As I survey the crowd below, especially my fellow veterans, I am extremely proud of myself — I really am — but I couldn't do it alone. I had help from above. I am overcome with a feeling of great gratitude, that I survived World War I — when I woke up each morning not knowing whether I would live or die — and that I could remember so many things in detail. Standing at the top of these stairs

is the ultimate moment of the whole trip, the successful culmination of many tributes and honours that have been paid to me recently.

"Did you know there was a doctor up there with you?" my son-in-law Ron Pike asks me as I reach the bottom of the stairs.

"I had no idea who he was," I reply. I never even saw him. Nor did I need him. I

TOP OF THE WORLD: Veterans Affairs Minister Fred Mifflin, Chief Warrant Officer Nick Zackaruk and I salute Canadian soldiers who died at Bourlon Wood during World War I.

Associated Press Photo

am humbled by my good fortune — again.

My name is Thomas Arnott Ballingal Spear — everybody calls me Tom — and I was born Oct. 22, 1896. By the grace of God, in the year 2000, I will have lived in three different centuries. I can honestly tell you that I have no major health worries and I've rarely been sick a day in my life. My doctor calls me a biological phenomenon.

In addition to serving in both world wars, I worked for the Canadian Pacific Railway for fifty years; enjoyed seventy and a half years of marriage with a marvelous wife, Margaret, who despite her passing still inspires me every day; and have a wonderful, loving family. My financial gain has also been enough to satisfy my necessities and pleasures comfortably.

I retired in 1963 (the year after my, ahem, ghost writer, Monte Stewart was born) but I still have my driver's license, maintain my own home, and participate in many sporting activities — including golf,

3

fishing and sometimes curling.

As you read further, I hope you will find the inspiration to enjoy every day — just as I do.

2

Making Memories

I returned to France — for the first time in eighty years — in April, 1997. It was my pleasure to accept an invitation from the Canadian government, in conjunction with the government of France, to help commemorate the 80th anniversary of the Battle of Vimy Ridge. That was the historic battle which, as one journalist covering the ceremonies wrote, "first stood Canada tall in the world's eyes."

Three thousand five hundred and ninety- eight Canadian soldiers died at Vimy in the name of freedom, ensuring the democracy which we still enjoy today. I will forever remember the kind words of Monsieur Pierre Paquini, France's Veterans Affairs Minister, as he addressed six of us veterans who had come for the ceremonies that April 9th day:

"I am here to tell you that Frenchwomen and Frenchmen have profoundly engraved in their memory those Canadian soldiers who came from so far away to spill their blood," he told us. "Be proud. Because, before this monument, for eighty years now, and for a longtime hereafter — forever, without a doubt — there will be women and men who will speak of Canadians."

Although I didn't serve at Vimy during the famous battle, France and Canada invited me to participate in, and sometimes lead, the ceremonies which were part of the annual pilgrimage. As I stood at the microphone, beneath the huge Vimy monument on a once ravaged battlefield that has been transformed into a lush green hillside, thousands of people from around the world — including my family, journalists,

military and government leaders — looked on as I read the Act of Remembrance in tribute to those who laid down their lives for their country.

"They shall grow not old as we who are left grow old," I told the crowd. "Age shall not weary them, nor the years condemn. At the going down of the sun, and in the morning, we shall remember them."

I was one of six World War I veterans, including two in wheelchairs, who agreed to travel overseas and be part of a physically demanding tour through France and Belgium, participating in two

SPECIAL VERSES: At the 80th anniversary of the Battle of Vimy Ridge, I read the Act of Remembrance in tribute to those who laid down their lives to preserve democracy.
Spear Family Photo

or three ceremonies each day in memory of our fallen comrades. I realized I was pretty darn lucky to be standing up there with those other veterans. It was a great lesson in humility. I thought, 'There but for the grace of God go I.' I also realized I'm one of the few that has lived

through a lot of war experiences and emerged without any disability.

I kept in contact with my war buddies for fifty or sixty years after our days in uniform together. But none of them was there that day. There's not one of them left. They're all dead. At home now, I look at my address book and wonder where these cherished old friends are. Tears come to my eyes. Why me? Why me? So many people have gone before and so many are sick right now and here I am running around enjoying every minute of life.

As I scanned the sea of faces that almost unbearably hot April day — men, women and children, young and old alike — I realized that I had an important story to share with others. Despite my age, and everything that I have done over the years, that Vimy trip greatly enhanced my life. If not for the invitation from the Canadian and French governments (for which I will always be extremely grateful) I doubt very much that I ever would have gone back to Europe.

During World War I, I lost my older brother Will. Until I made that trip back to France, I had never seen his grave. I wasn't quite sure whether I could handle the emotional part of seeing his tombstone and re-visiting so many sites which were destroyed during the war. (I still can't remember how I survived some of the deadliest situations.) But what I thought would be a painful experience actually made me a better person.

My daughters, Dorothy of Calgary (who was my official escort) and Joyce of Palo Alto, California, and their husbands Ron Pike and the late Shigeo Aoyagi, joined me on the journey. Dorothy and Joyce, who are now in their seventies, had heard several stories over the years about their Uncle Will but had never met him. They had never seen his grave either. One afternoon, when we had a break from the pilgrimage's official festivities, with some help from Canada's Veterans Affairs department, we discovered Will's final resting place. It's located in a triangle cemetery in a small town called Inchy-en-Artois.

We placed a picture plaque of Will, sealed by plastic, standing on stakes, into the ground. The plaque bears the inscription: "At last we

have returned to our youth, Will, dear brother and brave man whom we have loved these many years." It is signed by myself, Tom Spear, our brother Wallace Spear, my daughters, and their husbands.

Will's is just one of more than ninety graves in the cemetery bearing the names of deceased World War I veterans. All of the dead were casualties of battle at the Canal-du-Nord. The way I remember it from those many years ago, the site was just a machine-gunned mess. Today, however, tranquility reigns supreme.

What struck me most about our visit to his grave, and the entire Vimy pilgrimage, was the dramatic change from war to peace. I was anticipating something altogether different. During my tour of duty, everything was just devastated. Buildings were all broken down. Now everything on the French and Belgian countryside is beautifully marked off. Everything is in order. So tidy! The people say everything was just built up stone by stone again to what it once was. Small acreages and towns are just immaculate. The ravages of war have been replaced by the beauty of the land. It's just overwhelming. It really is.

On the Vimy site, you can see the trenches, you can see the potholes, and you can see the contour of the land. It's just a park now. The monument is very big, right on the very top of the ridge. You must be able to see for one hundred and fifty to two hundred kilometres from there on a clear day.

The trip intensified my already strong patriotism and love for my country. I realized I had played an important role in preserving the tremendous freedoms which we enjoy today. Perhaps more importantly, I also learned that there's hope for overcoming any disaster now. All it takes is love.

With my family there, I found it very easy to go back and relive some of those horrendous times of World War I. After the pilgrimage, I left France feeling that I had visited former scenes of desolation which are now peaceful and harmonious. Now, more than ever, I understand that life is very precious and every day is extremely gratifying. I now feel even more grateful for having the health I have and being able

to enjoy all the the things I do. My 1997 trip to Europe, which was paid in full by the Canadian government, was just one of the highlights of an extremely memorable year. It was among many events in my life between early 1996 and 1997 which sparked international media coverage and resulted in worldwide interest in my life.

In January of 1996, the Calgary Herald, namely Monte Stewart, published a feature article about me, reporting the renewal of my driver's licence at the age of ninety-nine. I was soon invit-

MEMORABLE MEDAL: The French government presented me with this medal as I participated in the 80th anniversary of the Battle of Vimy Ridge..

Calgary Herald Photo

ed to appear on the CBS Late Late Show with Tom Snyder in Hollywood.

A few weeks later, I received another all expenses paid trip, this time to New York City. It was my great honor to join other centenarians on the syndicated Donahue show just before it went off the air. It was an experiment designed to show North America what the elderly are capable of doing. I joined some prominent American seniors, who had excelled in spite of being over or near one hundred years of age. They were all tremendously inspiring.

One of the guests, Julius James, was one hundred and nine years old at the time. He appeared via satellite from his home in Tampa, Florida with his nephew Thomas James and great-great-great nephew. The state had ordered Julius out of his home, which he had inherited from his grandparents, Oliver and Queenie Habersham. They were slaves in

9

the 1800s. Julius, who suffered from cataracts and required a wheelchair, had steadfastly refused to move. A Florida court had ordered him to leave the premises so that a new interstate highway could come through his property. Sticking to his beliefs, Julius had turned down almost $2 million US for 8.5 hectares of his land. An appeals court judge later overturned the ruling and the state then scrapped its plans to build the highway.

Rev. Cloyce Copley of Ohio, one hundred at the time, who joined me in the studio, was invited to appear on the show after he had married his eighty- six year-old sweetheart. In World War I, he served as a U.S. Navy radio operator. He then became a Methodist minister for forty-two years. He was married to his first wife for seventy-two years!

Audrey Stubbart of Independence, Missouri, also one hundred at the time, was still working forty hours a week as a newspaper proofreader and columnist. She appeared via satellite from her newsroom.

"I think I can deal with anything," she says. "And I more or less have." She was among the homesteaders in the early 1920s. In 1916, Audrey, her husband and son and daughter left their native Iowa where, as a girl she had ground peanuts into peanut butter. They forged a new home in Wyoming. She overcame mandatory retirement age 65.

"I had more material," she jokingly told host Phil Donahue. He was amazed to hear that she had also coped through thirty-one years of widowhood.

Leola Peoples was also in the studio. A member of Donahue's crew brought out a cake in celebration of her one hundred and second birthday. She was among the first black women to graduate from medical school in Tennessee. She said that, because of her gender, she was forced to work as a waitress to make ends meet but she later got back into medicine, working as a nurse. (Movie star Elizabeth Taylor was one of her patients.) Leola retired from Columbia Presbyterian Hospital in New York in 1968. She couldn't recall the year exactly but knew it was the same year that U.S. civil rights leader Martin Luther King was assassinated.

Pauline Greer McLeve, one hundred at the time, flew to New York from her home state of Arizona. Still a stunning lady, she worked as a beautician for fifty years. Navaho indians used to come and watch her curl women's hair so that they could learn the techniques.

I demonstrated my golf swing for the studio audience and impressed Donahue with what he called my "washboard" stomach. "You are

YOUNG AT HEART

Fairy tales can come true, it can happen to you
If you're Young At Heart
For it's hard you will find to be narrow of mind
If you're Young At Heart.
You can go to extremes with impossible schemes,
You can laugh when your dreams
Fall apart at the seams and life gets
More exciting with each passing day,
And love is either in your heart or on its way.

SINGING IN THE YEARS: The words on this song sheet, Young at Heart, explain how I feel. This photo was taken at my 102nd Birthday, October 22, 1998.
Spear Family Photo

something, pal," he told me. "I'm serious. You are my inspiration."

There I was, a Canadian front and centre on a show that, in my view, often prided itself on being genuinely American. I wondered why Donahue's producers invited me. They may have felt Americans could identify with me, despite the fact that I'm a Canadian. (I must stress that am still very closely associated with the United States of America. Joyce and her family live there and I love that country almost as much as I love my own.)

I felt very secure and at home in front of Donahue's studio audience. I received the same affection that they showed the Americans appearing on the show. In all my experiences with the Donahue Show and

11

Tom Snyder Show, I was extremely proud to represent Canada on programs of that calibre. When Canadians found out that I had been on the Donahue show and Tom Snyder's show, it gave them pleasure to think that a Canadian did partake in American shows. They were amazed and seemed to be extremely pleased that I was chosen to represent Canada. I felt elated. Not everybody is chosen to appear on an American talk show. I think it's unique.

FUN WITH PHIL: After appearing on his show, talk show host Phil Donahue and I socialize off the set. In the background is Dr. Thomas Perls of Harvard University..
Spear Family Photo

Thanks to being introduced to Dr. Thomas Perls on the Donahue Show, my "kid" brother, Wallace, who is one hundred at the time of this writing, and I are also participating with other centenarians and their siblings in a tremendously important Harvard University study on aging. Dr. Perls tells me that our family, which has seen several of our loved ones live past ninety or one hundred, is "rare and extremely valuable from a genetics point of view."

Wallace and I have submitted tablespoonfuls of our blood for genetic analysis. We have also been interviewed extensively by medical experts as they attempt to discover how a person's background influences the aging process.

SALUTE TO VETERANS: After participating in Remembrance Day ceremonies at the Cenotaph in Ottawa, I salute all of those soldiers, including my dear late brother Will, who so valiantly gave their lives in battle.   Canadian Press Photo

Recent medical breakthroughs have discovered specific genes that appear to prevent age-related illness. The purpose of the study is to determine how centenarians and their siblings have achieved what the Harvard doctors describe as "extreme age". The Harvard research will be used to determine how these genes can help avoid such maladies as Alzheimer's disease, the incurable brain disease which afflicts hundreds of thousands of seniors worldwide. Hopefully, one day, the discoveries from our blood will help doctors understand the mysteries of why some people live longer than others.

Last February, I was featured in a Discovery Channel documentary entitled 100 Something. I've also made other television appearances on the Canadian Broadcasting Corporation's 50 and Up show, The Sports Network and locally in my hometown of Calgary. I have also been fea-

CANADIAN CAKE: Minister of Citizenship and Immigration Lucienne Robillard (left) helps new Canadian Kelly Ku, 9, while House of Commons Speaker Gilbert Parent instructs fellow First and Second World War veteran Roy Henley, 95, of Sidney, B.C. and myself during the citizenship ceremony.

Canadian Press Photo

tured on radio programs in Canada, the United States, and even South Africa, and in newspapers and magazines around the world.

In November of 1997, I received another invitation from the Canadian government. I was asked, and deeply honoured, to participate in citizenship and Remembrance Day ceremonies in Ottawa, our nation's capital.

On November 10, the day before Remembrance Day, I helped cut a cake resembling the Canadian flag as fifty immigrants from around the world were sworn in as our country's newest citizens. The occasion, organized by House of Commons speaker Gilbert Parent, marked the fiftieth anniversary of Canadian citizenship ceremonies and was televised live.

I was pleased that my grandson, Ned Worthington of California, accompanied me on these splendid occasions. He said that joining me in Ottawa was a great honour and made him very aware of the importance of being interested and involved in all of life's ceremonies.

CHATTING WITH THE CHIEF: Calgary police boss Christine Silverberg and I enjoy a pleasant conversation after lunch at the Bethany Care Centre in Calgary.
Calgary Herald Photo

On July 13, 1999, just before this book was published, I was bestowed with another honour as I was invited to speak at a luncheon at the Bethany Care Centre in Calgary. This luncheon paid tribute to some of us who are over one hundred. Much to my delight, Calgary police chief Christine Silverberg chatted with me afterwards.

These locally, nationally and internationally recognized events have made my whole life seem worthwhile. I now realize that, at my age, my excellent health and my activities are startlingly unique. I haven't lost any of my ambitions or desires. I can't explain exactly how I've managed to live so long but I do know what has made me feel so alive all these years. In coming pages, I'll tell you how I have gained immense inspiration from my positive attitude, faith, family, and healthy lifestyle.

As I take you back to some of the earlier times in my life, including some of the hardships (because, like everyone, our family are no strangers to tragedy and bereavement), I hope to show you how you can discover the joy of aging, enjoy a long and happy retirement, and

learn to love everything you do.

Believe me, I'm very proud of all the things I do. Even the cooking and cleaning! The title of this book, Carry On, reflects my ongoing commitment to excellence and endurance. I have two simple mottos: "If it's going to be, it's up to me!" and "You have to believe it to achieve it!"

I have also committed a short poem, entitled Age, to memory:

Age is a quality of time.
If you have left your dreams behind,
If love is cold,
If you no longer plan ahead,
If your ambitions all are dead,
Then you are old.
But —
If of life you make the best,
And in yourself you still feel zest,
If love you hold,
No matter how the birthdays fly,
No matter how the years go by,
You are not old.

This poem, whose author is unknown, symbolizes my life. In other words, I welcome the sunrise every day and the sunshine. What a difference the sun makes!

You see, my health is so damn good, really and truly, that I get up every morning looking forward to everything. I've got a positive outlook and I'm happy. I'm confident that I can do some good and go out every day with a smile on my face. I'm thankful for the day that's gone and eagerly anticipate the new day. I just can't express how thankful I am, how fortunate I am, and I'd like to pass on my good feelings to everybody.

I get all kinds of letters and cards from people of all ages saying, "You're a remarkable man". Do they stimulate me? You bet they do! They give me peace of mind and make me want to carry on and be a

model of good living, someone who's interested in all of life's experiences. Until recently, I never knew that I had accomplished so much just by talking about my long, good life. I had glimpses of that achievement at Bourlon Wood, Vimy Ridge and during my other public appearances at schools, seniors clubs and other special events. People in high places and the youth movement have told me the way they feel about how I conduct myself.

I spoke to a Grade 1 class recently at Woodbine Elementary School in Calgary and received cards back from every student. "Dear Mr. Spear," wrote a girl named Amy, "thank you for taking the time to see us and I'm sorry you lost so many friends in the war. You are a good man. Some day I wish I could be your friend."

Another student, Tristan Hatr, wrote: "I would like to be one hundred and one years old."

They're Grade 1 students! These and other words of praise give me great pleasure and inspiration. A lot of inspiration, I tell you. They have told me that I have done well and that I have succeeded in giving them instruction. If I can do it, so can you.

As you can probably tell, I'm a pretty happy man. This book is designed to help you get the most out of life and encourage you to carry on, under any circumstances, and be good citizens. It will also show you how to have a positive plan.

I think my book is a good story. It's not a millionaire's big deal. It's a happy story about a modest man. I like everything I do. I persevere in accomplishing what I set out to do. I know that I'm not going to live forever but I don't want my experiences to die with me. And I think you'll see that there'll be a lot of other people starting to get into the act and the idea of a good life.

I come from a humble family that had good health and maintained good ethics, ate good food, got lots of exercise and had a positive attitude. I love all the things I do. I've practised the theme of caring and doing things with excellence. It gets to be a habit — a good habit. It gives you great satisfaction to think that you can do anything as you

grow older.

Some people might say, "Well Tom, you're different. You're an exception. You can do it but I can't." What would I say to that? I don't think I'm unique. I don't think I'm a cocky guy. I think that other people can be like I am if they set their hearts and minds to it. You have to put something in it. If you do that, you'll get an awful lot out of life. I'd like to share my success and tell people that anything is possible. So, carry on reading.

3

Forming an Attitude

My attitude is my driving force. People often ask me how I manage to stay so positive, especially after the tragedy I have witnessed over the years. I give the most credit to my father and mother, who I believe, were ahead of their time around the start of the twentieth century. I never heard my mother and father say a cross word to each other and their teachings, along with the priceless tutoring of my late wife Margaret, continue to guide me.

I get great satisfaction and happiness from my attitude. It has helped me become a good father, family man, and loyal to my country and God. I discovered that you must not always look inward. You must avoid dwelling on your bad experiences, the sad times and the tragedies that come to all of us. You must learn and carry on, looking outward and upward.

Our family — which included Dad, Mother, my grandmother and my brothers and sister — was a tightly knit group. We took pride in whatever responsibilities were assigned. I think now that this early in-home instruction was a governing factor that has always motivated me in all work undertaken. Coupled with that inborn urge to do things well was the satisfaction and happiness we had from performing to a certain standard.

This sense of pride in achievement, joy in success, however humble, and the high level of Christian endeavour were qualities that I still retain to this day. As you'll discover as you continue reading, my father and mother set the stage for the paths we were to follow. The goals

were defined, the expectations great. We were really blessed to have parents that were dedicated to improvement and progress. Mother and Dad were great leaders, wherever they went. They stressed honesty, integrity, religious beliefs, love, faithfulness, morality and patriotism.

My father, David Spear, born in 1854, was the third child in a family of thirteen born to William and Sarah Spear in Cobourg, Ontario. From Scotland they brought with them the skills of farming, raising mostly fruits and vegetables in the new country. Everyone had to work and everyone had to go to school.

David determined early that his career would be in the ministry. He was a splendid teacher. He gave an awful lot of time to teaching, educating kids and encouraging them. I have heard him tell of summers spent picking cotton in Arkansas to bring back the needed funds for the tuition. He graduated from Knox College in Toronto, Ontario with a B.A. in theology.

Soon after accepting this ministry, he and my mother were married in Toronto and went to Innisfail, which is now part of the Province of Alberta. He was the first ordained minister between Calgary and Edmonton and, thus, had charges in Olds, Bowden and Red Deer, as well as Innisfail. Dad's name is listed in the church record and he became quite famous for his early ministry there.

If you have ever visited those towns, located on vast and mostly uninhabited prairie, you would experience gentle summers, but very hard winters. Dad rode a horse alone on many of his missions. I look at his wedding picture and see this fine looking man with black hair and moustache, a healthy complexion and a gleam in his eye. One might wonder why he chose such difficult and challenging places when his education, his appearance, and a talented and educated wife would have been such assets in more populated, comfortable environments. Now I know. His ideas about bringing up a growing family were paramount.

I don't think Dad ever had very much of a bank account. We were taught to live independently. His surroundings allowed him to teach us

how to hunt, fish, plant and harvest. I do believe my father loved the country life. He loved his calling, he wanted adventure and he had the pioneering spirit to overcome hardship.

And then there was my mother. Margaret Helen Ballingal was also from Eastern Canada. She was born in 1861 in Stratheden, Ontario,

PIONEER PARENTS: This photo of my father, Rev. David Spear and mother Margaret Helen Ballingal Spear was taken on their wedding day, June 6, 1894 in Innisfail, Alberta.

Spear Family Photo

the second child of Thomas and Agnes Ballingal. There was one son, whose name I bear along with my grandfather Ballingal. My mother was well educated and musically talented. Before she was married, she taught piano at the Toronto Conservatory of Music. In addition to her artistic abilities, she was an adventurous woman, the daughter of adventurous parents. Mother had that pioneering spirit too.

Their first child was born with the assistance of a veterinarian. It was not an easy birth, but my brother, William David Spear, was the happy result on March 28, 1895. For her next child, my mother returned to her mother's home in Galt, Ontario. I, Thomas Arnott Ballingal Spear, was born on October 22, 1896.

Three years later, Dad accepted a call from Balcarres, Saskatchewan, and from there we went to Pipestone, Manitoba.

The family continued to grow. Robert Wallace Spear, whom I affectionately call my kid brother although he's approaching one hundred,

was born March 31, 1899 and my sister, Agnes Helen Spear, entered the world on June 7, 1903.

My parents were self-sufficient but not wealthy. We did not have a lot of money to spend. Our father and mother taught us how to live frugally. We had to make do with what we had. There were no cars. We travelled locally by horse and buggy. They eventually had rubber tires on them in the city and all you could hear was the click, clack, click, clack of the horses'

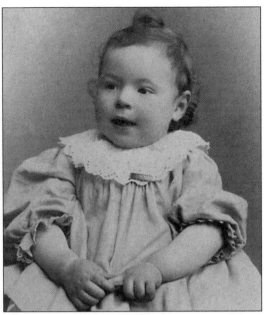

WEE WILL: My brother Will was one and a half years old in this photo, taken at Paris, Ontario. In those days, it was common for baby boys to wear dresses. Spear Family Photo.

hooves on the pavement. Seats were all leather. Some of the carriages would have the top down, like a sportscar.

As is still the case today, all transportation vehicles were made in eastern Canada. We did all our own repairs. There was pride in everything that you did. You had to grease the wheels and that type of thing. A wheel was made up of so many wooden spokes. To travel long distances, you had to take the train.

There were no indoor toilets either because there was no modern plumbing. When we had to go, we went in outhouses. Even the hotels would have outhouses. Everyone had two-holers, or two seats, or one-holers. Some of the outhouses just had big sliding drawers. You had to pull them out with horses.

If you had to get up at night to go to the bathroom, you would sit on a pot. Some people used old catalogues as toilet paper. You never saw soft paper ever. We never bought any toilet paper that I could ever

remember. There was no sewage system in the town. Anybody that had sewage treatment would have septic tanks. Some of the more affluent people had them.

You had to get your own drinking and wash water from the river, wells, pumps or ice. We dug our own wells by hand and, once we struck water, reinforced the well with wood or cement. We also had ice houses that stored the ice, packed in sawdust, in summer and melted it. You just got it out of the ice house and put it on the boiler on the stove. It was a big job.

On wash day, you always had a big boiler with ice in it in the back of the stove. We (mostly Mother and Grannie) washed clothes by hand with a scrubbing board and a bucket.

When it was time for a bath, you had to heat the water on the stove and put it in the bathtub. Two or three of us kids at a time then splashed around in it.

Everything was dependent on water. That's why the towns in the country were built as close as possible to Red River, Roseau River or their tributaries.

Water was also essential for the railways because it was required for the steam engines. Electricity wouldn't become prevalent in Manitoba until the 1920s.

Some might consider this way of life hard but we didn't think anything of it. It was part of living. It gave you a deep appreciation of progress. (People should understand how people lived in our earlier days.) You felt a sense of accomplishment. You were inspired to have a better way to live, an easier way of living, and more leisure time.

This mentality is still with me. It's instilled in me. It's an inspiration to improve.

Mother and Dad were our tutors, always present and always attentive to our particular needs. They had a marvelous faith in God and thus our home education was based on the Bible teachings, by which we also lived. My parents were the leaders in the towns and the communities where they served and we as "the preacher's kids" were taught to

conduct ourselves properly.

However, we did not always live up to that high standard and, at times, were dubbed "the worst kids in town." One time my brother Will was late coming home from a rabbit hunt in the woods. We were all in a great state of fear as there were rifles in the group. He finally arrived at the manse property. There, he was met by my dad, who was holding a whip which he later applied liberally.

I took exception to the punishment and ran out and kicked my dad in the shins. The result of that was a real good dose of the whip for me too. Mother intervened but I still received the same punishment as Will: restrictions from any sporting activities for a long time. Dad, in later years, recalled the incident and confessed that he was proud of me that day.

Our love, respect and deep devotion to Mother and Dad were never in doubt. Our Dad was always our hero and best friend. His counselling and help with our schooling was a very pleasurable part of our early days and throughout our school years. His own university days held him in good stead and then there was his library at our disposal. There were encyclopedias, reference books, and collections of prose and poetry which were certainly not available to many of our schoolmates.

We had our own libraries too, set up meticulously and well indexed for loans to our friends. Our favourite books in the early years were: The Boy's Own Annual, all of the Horatio Alger success stories, the G.A. Henty series, the histories of Great Britain in all her glory such as, With Roberts in Pretoria, With Kitchener in Sudan, With Clive in India and With Wolfe in Quebec and many more. These books, of course, may have influenced our patriotic tendencies and also shaped our desire to excel.

We also tried to get a Jack Harkaway series into our shelves but Dad banned them because he judged them "unacceptable" for young and active minds.

In this atmosphere, we started to school and I remember my first day with great clarity. My brother, Will, a year older, was already at school

and had such great tales to tell that I wanted to experience those same exciting events and get into school homework too. One summer evening Dad took me to see the principal, Miss Calder, who lived nearby. After a few questions which I apparently answered with assurance, she said I was an acceptable candidate for Grade 1.

So, on my first day, I went off to the halls of learning in the charge of my older brother. I was really eager as I lined up with the scholars from grades one to ten and marched in line to the classroom. We went through roll call and registration and then we lined up and paraded into another room.

There, to my growing apprehension, was a doctor at a table with assistants. It dawned on me that that was a medical inspection of some kind. In fact, it was a mandatory inoculation. As the line progressed, I realized this was not going to be pleasant. When my turn came to advance, I turned, ran out the door and rushed home into Dad's study, bawling like a baby. Mother, concerned, tried to console me, but they both agreed this was a necessary part of getting into school. So back to school I went with Dad. The doctor duly vaccinated me. (I still have the scar on my left arm to prove it.) Little did I realize that I would be jabbed and probed a good many times in the army and air force.

My school days began in Pipestone, Manitoba. I can recall many memorable events that occurred there. Our manse, across the street from the Presbyterian church where my father officiated, was surrounded by a large field and meadow full of gophers and mice. We kept ourselves busy snaring these pests or trying to drown them out. We didn't make much of an impression on the animal world — but we tried.

I recall terrific snowfalls in that town. The roadway that separated the house from the church was, at times, buried underneath huge snowbanks. Will and I made a tunnel through the snow to the church. What an undertaking that was! It has remained in my memory all of my life.

About this time, my grandmother, Agnes Laird Ballingall, came to live with us. Widowed at the age of sixty-four, she became an integral part of our household for the next forty years until her death at the age

of one hundred and four. She was a tremendously active, gentle Christian woman — highly regarded by all. She was my mother's mother, but both my parents respected and loved her and were grateful for her very kind and skillful help in the home.

She was a great comfort to us, her adoring grandchildren, and I will always remember her joyful ways. We always had an ally in Grannie.

When Will and I managed to get together in a dugout during World War I, we talked about the childhood memories that were dear to us. The making of that tunnel through the snow, the gophers in the field, the firecrackers under tin cans on Dominion Day (now known as Canada Day), July 1, were happy recollections.

We talked too of Lieut. Col. Rattray, commanding officer of Tenth Batallion on our front. He was a member of Dad's congregation in Pipestone. He was a successful merchant and the officer in charge of a militia group in peaceful times in that area. His daughter, an only child, was a real tomboy. He restricted her active life by tethering her on a long rope so she could not run away. That was the talk of the town, of course. Still, this fine soldier was loved by all his men of all ranks and went into action with them. His promotion to brigadier general was a popular one, but it took him away from his beloved batallion. I was later to receive considerable assistance from him.

Then there was the time the grain elevators burned down. Classes were dismissed and we all ran down to the Canadian Pacific Railway station to watch the grain spilling like oil out of the bins as the elevator tumbled down.

The station stands out in my memory for another reason. I remember the return of three veterans from the Boer War. The smoke of the approaching train in the distance and the arrival of these brave men in their scarlet tunics was extremely impressive. Imagining their feats of valour, we cheered as they stepped off the train. The British Empire and her concerns were always very close to us because we were a part of it.

At Pipestone, we had three horses, a cow, two or three pigs, several cats and a good, faithful dog. We were all farm-oriented and had

learned how to harness the team of Elgin and Beryl. One day, Will and I went hunting with Dad in a democrat carriage behind our two fine ponies. Out in the field, Dad spotted a prairie chicken in flight, stood up in the buggy and fired a shot. The horses, startled by the loud bang, jerked forward and sent me tumbling out of the carriage and one of its light wheels rolled over me. I jumped out and shouted, more than once, "I'm not dead yet!"

Then there were the sleigh and buggy rides with Mother and Dad to the Indian reserves, where Dad conducted church services. In summer, it was a treat to get out to the small villages. Mother played the organ and one of us was sure to be along for the ride. In winter, we took the large sleigh and used hot bricks wrapped in cloth as foot warmers and two or three real buffalo robes. We were always glad to get back to the warm manse fired by wood burning stoves. Grannie always welcomed us home with hot cups of tea.

Dad was quite popular with the Indians from both reserves in his pastoral area and often these folks would come to town sporting Indian dress and moccasins. When we came home from school, we often found Indians sitting in front of the kitchen stove, smoking long-stemmed pipes and keeping warm. We had no fear of them and Grannie was always the generous hostess to these people she loved. What I remember most is the terrible stench of the leather moccasins drying out.

I am not sure that Mother liked these visits but she apparently viewed them as part of her responsibility as the home's angel — which she was. We, the children, loved these visits and became really good friends with "Dad's indians" and even learned some sacred songs in their language. (I recall a few lines from Jesus Loves Me.)

The Canadian government paid these treaty Indians an annual stipend but, as part of the deal, they were prohibited from drinking spirits or possessing liquor. Yet, local politicians, in a bid to get the Indian vote, often organized gala powwows where they could eat and drink merrily. The powwow festivities, featuring splendid costumes and

feather headdresses, always drew a crowd.

Dad took me to one powwow where he spotted a couple of his parishioners partying. He carried a big white scroll with immense seals depicting the authority of the Canadian government, which could cancel their treaty payments if they participated in the drinking and carousing. When they saw the intimidating seals, they packed up and headed back to the reserve.

Each powwow, with dancing and chanting that grew louder and more lively, really excited me. Just another day at the office for my dad though.

In the summer of 1904, Dad received a call from a town called Holland, east of Pipestone on the same branch of the CPR. At that time, Will was eight, I was seven going on eight, Wallace five and Helen almost two. Dad and Mother decided to accept that call and we prepared to leave. On a bright sunny day, the townspeople, several Indians and the Pipestone Band bid us farewell. As the passenger train pulled in and we boarded the coaches, people shouted in unison "God Be With You Until We Meet Again." The train pulled away but the voices followed us, reminding us of happy days and old friends.

In Holland, in keeping with tradition, a crowd greeted us and escorted us to the manse which stood on what I, as a kid, thought was a very high hill. The Presbyterian church was on the brow of the hill next to the house. The home was spacious with enough bedrooms to accommodate our family of seven, including Grannie. But the hill stands out more in my mind. Running, from top to bottom for about half a mile (or what's known as a kilometre these days), right through the centre of town, it was excellent for sled rides in winter.

I believe Holland is the first place I had a hockey stick in my hand. We had a homemade ice rink in the big vacant lot east of the manse. Everybody who wanted to skate hauled water from wells to help make the ice. A lot were interested because the covered rink in town was used for skating only — and we had other games in mind.

One family, the Lipsetts, had an excellent rink in their backyard. I

recall the rink very well, not only because the Lipsetts were good friends but because I lost a front tooth in a hockey game there. That was a real tragedy, in days when dentists practised only in cities, and a source of worry for a minister with a small stipend and four children. I eventually got a peg-like tooth to fill the gap. This did not deter me in any way from playing hockey, which was my main sport for more than thirty years.

I believe Mr. Lipsett was also the commanding officer of the volunteer militia. Canada did not have a standing army in those days but reservists were very active in peacetime. When World War I started, this same Mr. Lipsett became a colonel and then a general in the Canadian army and served on the front line where I was stationed. He was loved by his men.

During an inspection tour at the front, a sniper shot and killed him. I remember the funeral of this brave man and friend. Thousands attended the funeral, held in broad daylight a short distance behind the front under the watchful eye of enemy posts. It was a fitting tribute for the splendid and brave general who rests there today. We saw a German observation plane fly over our huge assembly. Some soldiers said it dropped a wreath in the area. The enemy abstained from artillery fire, although we were well within range of their guns. The Germans probably knew who was being laid to rest.

Such seemingly unexpected tributes happened occasionally. When a Canadian airman shot down the Red Baron behind our lines, we allowed the German planes to fly over and drop wreaths. The Canadian pilot credited with this great victory was Roy Brown. I came to know Roy's family, who lived in Winnipeg, after the war.

After a year in the ministry in Holland, Dad, who was earning about seven hundred dollars a year, felt he had to make ends meet for his rapidly growing children. He purchased a hardware store and operated it profitably for a year. We moved from the manse to a suite above the store.

Will and I liked to help Dad in his store duties. Putting glass in bro-

ken windows with putty was one of the jobs I liked best. Later, when I had broken windows or doors, I repaired them using the same skills I had learned in Holland.

Later that year, Dad accepted an offer to join a real estate firm in Winnipeg. Now, we were in a big city, established in a two-storey home at 185 Cathedral Avenue, close to schools and church. Dad liked the work and both he and Mother became very active in church and community affairs, along with our dear Grannie.

Will and I went to McCrae School on North Main, about a mile away from our home. I was in Grade 5 and can remember my teacher, Miss Fox. She rapped my knuckles a few times for not finishing my writing exercises with an upward stroke. She was a nice looking lady and was very popular with my parents and other students.

The school principal was another matter. A large man, with bright red hair, he lived up to everything those looks implied. He oversaw everything and used the strap for petty infringements. On one occasion, he decided to administer the strap to a friend of mine for talking in class. He did this in the hall, enabling everyone to hear the boy's cries. No sooner had I jumped out of my seat to head after him than Miss Fox ordered me to sit down. I vowed to get even with that big bully but I never got the chance. He was transferred to another school.

There was also some military training in the city schools. An officer, Col. Billman, came regularly and marched us all over the playgrounds in army formation. Boy, I never thought I could be a soldier, but I found out differently!

At McCrae School, we played lacrosse and soccer against other schools and I cracked the lineups of both teams.

In addition to the school playgrounds, we had a large area behind our home on Cathedral Avenue, where we played our games in organized groups. St. John's College also had cricket fields that we used occasionally.

Part of our school curriculum at McCrae included a manual training class at Norquay School. This was a favourite class of ours. Tools

always intrigued me and here there were wonderful, shiny new tools and instructors. The teachers required a plan for each project and you were expected to complete that plan. I continue to be interested in woodworking. Will also was tremendously interested in this craft and became very skilled before enlisting in the army.

Our best friends were the Polsons, an old Winnipeg family who were among the earliest settlers in the north end. Mr. and Mrs. Polson had two boys, Alec and Hugh. Both boys were university students and brilliant scholars. Hugh was at law school while Alec studied electrical and mechanical engineering. They also lived on Cathedral Avenue and had a shed barn where they made things and conducted experiments. They welcomed us and shared their intriguing plans. One experiment harnessed steam power with boiling water in tin cans. We cut small holes in the cans and put spinners on top so that the released steam would whirl them.

Alec went on to invent a special built-in switch that could direct a streetcar. Until then all streetcar drivers had to get out of their vehicles and move the switch manually.

A California-based electrical company hired Alec in the 1920s. He married a Miss Diamond who had also lived on our street. Strangely, Alec disappeared from a beach and has never been found.

We also knew two sisters, Martha and Gertrude Hutchinson. They came to visit wherever we were. Gertrude an artist, painted beautiful water colours. She gave our family some of her lovely floral works and they still decorate our homes today.

Perhaps I put an end to our Winnipeg days. I had learned to ride a bicycle there and Dad forbade me from riding farther south than the CPR subway. I broke that rule — and the bike's handlebars — once. That was Dad's transportation to work. I guess he thought it was time to get to the country, creating a little more room for his active sons and daughter.

Since his heart was still in the ministry, he accepted an offer in 1907 to take over the Presbyterian Church in Dominion City and three out-

CLASS ACT: I'm the one on the right end, front row in this photo of my Sunday school class, taken at Dominion City, circa 1907. Will is in the back row, third from left.

Spear Family Photo

lying charges. This was a town of about six hundred, about sixty-five miles south of Winnipeg on the CPR line to Minneapolis/St. Paul, Minnesota.

A fast passenger train ran daily between Canada and the United States. Two other mixed trains carrying both passengers and freight, travelled between Winnipeg and the border town of Emerson.

We arrived, along with Grannie, in Dominion City on Halloween and received a rousing welcome from church and town dignitaries. We had arrived at our home.

With Dad back behind the pulpit, Mother playing the church organ, our lives would be molded together here. We became a strong, united family. The next six years in Dominion City provided my fondest childhood memories. Our school, church and social activities were more permanent. Undoubtedly, Dad had researched the educational and religious opportunities thoroughly before he accepted his call to the church and its affiliates. Our home, the manse of the Presbyterian church, was

a large two-storey dwelling, six blocks from church and about 10 blocks from school. The school taught grades one through twelve and we played baseball and soccer on the open fields nearby.

Mother baked eight loaves of bread — plus rolls — each week. Their wonderful fragrances met us when we came home from school.

The Roseau River served as the source of our recreational activities in summer and winter. Located one hundred yards from our barn, it was the popular scene of swimming and fishing in summer and skating and curling in winter. Summertime was rivertime in D.C. We had several favorite swimming holes, all deep enough to be dangerous. Parents and teachers obeyed an unwritten rule requiring a lifeguard to be appointed for each swimming session, someone who could swim well and also be responsible and trustworthy. A year before we arrived in D.C., a young boy named Jimmy Lawson drowned.

Will was usually the one in charge of our afternoon romps to the river. No one questioned his ability as a guard. He saved at least two lives.

One swimming hole, known as the Duck Pond, was particularly dangerous and closely patrolled. There was an island in the centre and you had to swim a hundred yards to reach it safely. We considered the Duck Pond the ultimate test. One day, Cyril Wallace failed. We had all peeled off our clothes and raced into the water after somebody gave the usual starting signal: "Last one in is a stinker!"

Seeing that Cyril was in trouble, Will dived in and pulled him up to the water's surface. Cyril said I saved him but I just happened to be there and helped bring him home to Mother and a warm bed.

Cyril had come to Canada from England after friends sponsored his emigration. He worked in a bank owned by a wealthy Englishman named William Mortlock. Cyril spent many hours at our home and eventually moved in with us until the start of World War I. Will and I would serve with him on the French and Belgian battlefields.

As I mentioned earlier, we also fished in our old friend, the Roseau, using rods made from long, slim, willowy branches, lines of string and

hooks with worms. We caught several catfish but they were not considered edible. (How times have changed. Today, people consider catfish a delicacy.) Dad taught us how to fillet the fish and our cats and dogs benefitted from our fun.

In winter, we devised rinks on the river by chopping holes in the ice and flooding them. We skated with many of our schoolmates. At night, we built big bonfires of branches, logs, flotsam and anything else combustible, and put on our skates in bitterly cold weather. Then off we skated down the ice, away from the light and warmth. That was scary but part of the fun.

When the river froze over before a snowfall, we battled against wind and time and tried to skate to the junction of the Roseau and the Red.

We also made curling rinks by shovelling snow and flooding smaller portions of the river. We strived to make the area fairly smooth. Each curling sheet was seventy-five yards long and four yards wide, with snow banks on each side. We made hacks and colored circles for the house. We made our rocks from blocks of wood with large spikes serving as handles. We all had our own pair of rocks, adorned them with paint and fancy handles and took them home after the match.

The town had an indoor curling rink, where Dad played. Later in our youth, we had a Spear rink — three boys and their dad. It was great to play with granite stones.

We read about curling in the Winnipeg Free Press, which we received daily from the city. The presses rolled at four o'clock in the morning and arrived at our home three hours later.

In 1916, while I was serving overseas in the army, the Roseau crested along its banks. In 1965, the Roseau and the Red overflowed, carried our old home off its foundations, and almost completely destroyed it. Fortunately, Mother was living in Winnipeg at that time and Dad had passed away in 1948. The flood stemmed from the overflow of the mighty Mississippi River in the United States and spanned north of the border as far as Winnipeg and Brandon.

The flood which struck Manitoba in 1996, as the Red and Roseau

again overflowed, reminded me of that earlier incident.)

The number one priority, wherever we moved, was the arrangement of Dad's library. It was his pride and joy and he meticulously arranged and documented the encyclopedias, dictionaries and mathematics books that were within easy reach from his desk. The desk, always well polished with items stowed safely, was a rolltop that also came with us wherever we moved. He carefully filed and documented his religious notes and kept his Bible close at hand.

Although just a year older, Will protected me wherever we went — and I guess I needed a lot of help at times.

Mother and Dad participated in all aspects of the town's church and social life. They led children's activities in the church, the Ladies' Aid, the Christian Temperance Society and always provided understanding counselling to those in trouble. All of our family signed the church's pledge to abstain from alcohol and tobacco for life.

Most of the Sunday School students signed it too. It was an important step for me. I have honoured that pledge to this day and, I believe, I owe much of my good health and long life to it. God gave me a wonderfully healthy body, a good mind and a strong desire to live up to our Bible teachings.

We had fine role models in our parents and grandmother, who inspired us to live honourably and morally, and who gave us years of guidance and provided a secure and loving childhood. Those years formed the basis for my journey through life. I am still proud to acknowledge God and let Him direct my paths.

Dad had three outlying charges: Woodmore, seven miles (or about eleven kilometres) east of Dominion City; Newbridge, seven miles northeast of D.C. and Arnaud, eight miles (or thirteen kilometres) north on the CPR line. About fifty people comprised the congregation, including children for Sunday School, and a choir of about eight or ten. Afternoon services alternated between Arnaud, Woodmore and Newbridge.

The dirt roads, often muddy or buried underneath snow, prompted

Dad to create his own mode of transportation to Arnaud on the rail line. With permission from CPR officials, and the aid of a tripod that secured his bicycle wheels to the rails, he peddled off to his services as town residents often watched in wonder. On a good day with no wind, he could make the trip from D.C. to Arnaud in about 20 minutes. He forbade us children from using it. In all my years with the CPR, I would never see another device like it. I saw hand- pumped cars, but no other bikes. He never had a single mishap.

Transportation became a major concern, so we bought two horses and rented a large stable near the Roseau River. This river flows westward and drains into the Red River, about fifteen miles (or twenty kilometres) west of Dominion City. We used the Roseau's then clear and pure water for drinking, washing dishes, bathing and ice. We watered our horses and cows at a trough.

By this time, we were old enough to be assigned chores. Will fed, watered and curried our horses and cleaned the barn. I milked two cows each morning. Will and I would start out at half past seven each morning and return home for a good, hot breakfast of rolled oats with lots of cream and milk.

We had two cats and several kittens, whom we cuddled up with at night. These little dollies would follow me down the path through a big garden (snow banks in winter). When I started milking, they would sit up and I would squirt milk from the cow's udder into their gaping mouths — straight from factory to consumer. They were my morning friends for many years.

These good years still inspire me. Our activities from age nine to fourteen ranged from strictly supervised school work to Bible studies. We also played hockey, soccer and baseball and also enjoyed swimming.

Any misconduct, from flippancy to elders to swearing or fighting, led to penalties. Dad served as both judge and jury. His standard penalty: "Go to the study and memorize two pages of catechism." We dreaded those words because they took us away from the games we loved.

Mother played the role of peacemaker and provided the base of Dad's power and strength in difficult times. She commanded us troops when Dad was away. Her ultimate punishment was a mouthful of mustard.

Along with horses, cows, pigs and hens, we had a faithful black Newfoundland dog named Cap. Trained as a watchdog and cattle herder, he was our vital sleigh dog in winter. With a harness provided by the local saddler, he pulled one hundred pound sacks of flour home from the grain elevator on a runner sled. In summer, he hauled kids on a heavy duty wagon.

There was a Dr. Robertson in our town, who had two young sons with whom we sometimes played. The younger one, Bruce, liked to pass by our house and irritate Cap by running a stick long the fence. Cap obliged by barking and snarling when the stick came in contact with his nose. We warned Bruce and asked him to stop teasing Cap. When that didn't work, Dad asked Dr. Robertson to speak to Bruce.

However, Bruce persisted and we had to tie Cap up if he came within fifty yards of the manse. We were afraid an open gate could spell danger. One day our fear became reality. Along came Bruce and Cap jumped the fence and knocked him down. Cap didn't bite him or hurt him but scared little Bruce ran home and told his father that the minister's dog had attacked him on public property. Dr. Robertson threatened to sue if we didn't get rid of Cap. Townfolk were in an uproar because they loved Cap too.

Dad, because of the threat of the law, decided to put Cap down. There could be no lawsuit in the family of a minister, he said. I cannot describe how heartbroken and sad we all were. When we moved across the river, we acquired a sheep collie, who was a good dog too, but no pet could match our love for Cap.

By 1911, Dad realized he needed another income to provide for the family and cover post-secondary educational expenses. He and mother purchased a quarter section (one hundred and sixty acres) of farm land, about a mile out of town on the north side of the Roseau, for one dollar per acre. They also bought a nearby lot for a home, barn and out-

houses. On the farmland, we planned to grow grain for sale and use our home's garden for our personal consumption. Mr. Robert Hempton, the town carpenter, drew up plans for the barn and home. Dad, Will, Wallace and I built a comfortable cottage with four bedrooms upstairs and two on the main floor. My siblings and I slept on the top floor and Mother, Dad and Gran had beds on the main floor. The dining room, living room and big kitchen filled the rest of the main floor. In the dirt-lined basement, we stored fruits and vegetables. The basement's wood-burning stoves and pipes heated the home in winter. The barn accommodated four or five horses, a couple of cows, hens and other small farm animals.

In the summers before our home was completed, Will and I worked for local farmers living outside Dominion City. We couldn't wait for July to come around so that we could get out of school and go farming for two months. Usually, we went to Wallace Arthur's farm. It was a big operation with fifteen horses, ten cows and countless pigs and hens. It was quite a responsibility to care for the livestock and then hitch up the teams of large horses to harvest the crops. We found it exciting to be behind the mower cutting the hay or on another machine raking the grass and arranging it in windrows to be stoked for drying out.

We had good sleeping accommodations in their spacious farmhouses, where we also ate hearty and delicious meals. The young girls in the family brought our lunches out to the fields.

I don't remember getting paid, but maybe we did. We learned to do many things that helped us on our own farm but, primarily, we just enjoyed interesting, happy days living with generous folk who gave us memorable experiences to cherish.

The new home made a great difference in our lives for we were some distance from the ice rinks, playing fields and our former neighbours. Our whole daily routine had changed now that we were part of a farm operation.

As we grew older, our education dominated our father's plans and we worked hard to head our classes. I did sometimes but a girl named

Kathleen Ginn usually finished ahead of me. Kathleen was clever, bright and pretty. She won all the spelling bees and was a whiz at math. (She was also my sweetheart, but the war, and fate apparently, would intervene. Kathleen became an honor student and attained her teaching credential in Winnipeg. When I was overseas, she sent me wonderful packages of food, which I shared with my chums. We corresponded for two years but lost contact when I was posted to the front. Kathleen married a fine gentleman and successful farmer, Fred Empson, and moved into a home near Emerson, where I settled after the war. Alas, both Kathleen and her first baby died in childbirth. It was an extremely sad time for our families. I will never forget her.)

Will and I were now in high school, Wallace and Helen were in what's now known as junior high and new interests began to emerge. Helen shared in our plans and kept up with us.

One of our chums had left home recently and gone to a telegraphy school. Within the year, he landed a job as a CPR agent in a small town in Saskatchewan, which seemed a far away place to us at that time. Since it was rumored he was earning good money, we became interested and built telegraphy sets in the house, from upstairs to downstairs. The CPR agent in Dominion City, one of Dad's good friends, encouraged us by allowing us to listen in on the wire at the train station. After hours of practice, we became really good, or so we thought. This activity would literally spark my lifelong interest in telegraphy.

Will decided he wanted to study horticulture and was going to attend the University of Manitoba's agricultural college in Winnipeg. Wallace wanted a career in banking and Helen intended to obtain her teaching credential. I was slated for higher education — but other circumstances intervened.

Still in school, I began spending many hours by the train station window listening to the messages moving between Winnipeg and St. Paul, Minnesota, quite a fast circuit with the "cut-in" and "sounder" switch on. I think Mr. Lawson, the agent, left it on deliberately, so that I could hear it from the window, even after station hours. I stayed there and

successfully read a lot of the information that moved over the wire. I hung around that station every chance I could.

In 1912, opportunity knocked. Mr. Lawson's assistant was promoted and transferred to a station outside of Winnipeg. Mr. Lawson invited me to apply for the vacant spot. Thanks to his help, and likely recommendation, I started work on July 8, 1912. I was fifteen years old, with Grade 11 completed.

My duties, as defined by Mr. Lawson, required me to meet Train 225 each morning at seven, load freight and baggage and complete billing paperwork. Train 225 ran daily, except Sunday, between Emerson and Winnipeg. Another train ran between St. Paul, Minn. and Winnipeg, but that did not stop. Each night at seven o'clock, the southbound Train 226 pulled into Dominion City and I unloaded express baggage and way freight.

My twelve-hour shift between seven in the morning and seven at night passed quickly. I spent my leisure time fixing in on the fast wireless circuits, but couldn't copy the messages fast enough. I used one of my first pay cheques to buy a manual Oliver typewriter. After many hours of practice, I managed to type the messages as they came over the wire. The Oliver stood me in good stead when positions requiring typewriter skills were advertised.

I also learned accounting and CPR bookkeeping rules. Travelling auditors, who could step off the train and do a spot check any time, kept strict tabs on our books. (The CPR would maintain that method throughout my fifty-year career. My books never showed any shortages.)

As my life at home was changing, I looked for something better than my fifteen-dollar monthly salary. I gave Mother ten dollars for room and board and paid off the typewriter with the rest. Heavy wartime traffic created some new jobs and my superiors asked me to write up my rulebook to be eligible for a relief train order position. I studied the rulebook and memorized important directions required for train operations. Soon, chief dispatcher Mr. E.G. Trump called me into Winnipeg

to take a train operations exam.

The imposing Mr. Trump, or E.G.T. as he was known to telegraphers who viewed him as a god, was kind and friendly to me. I wore short pants, and long black stockings, the garb of a schoolboy. I was amazed by the office where all trains were dispatched. Batteries of sounders and relays, operated by skilled telegraphers, sang out their dots and dashes. I never dreamed that one day I would be sitting at those same desks fulfilling those same urgent duties.

I passed the exam and met other dispatchers, some of whom I would meet again in 1923. At the end of that memorable day, Mr. Trump kindly suggested that I wear long pants if I was called upon to move.

I was now a telegrapher and started my seniority on July 2, 1913, by relieving the station agent at Arnaud for a couple of days. In late July, I was sent to Franklin on the Minnedosa subdivision. I operated a train turnaround station at Ameer, an uninhabited location sporting simply a boxcar with a stove, table, bunk and telegraph desk. Pusher engines assisted trains up a steep three-mile hill out of Minnedosa's terminal and I would receive orders for their return. These orders served as a safety feature in single-track train operations, ensuring the pusher engines returned to the terminal after they helped the main train. Crews brought supplies that I requested from Minnedosa. After two months of total isolation, I was ready for the night operator position at Neepawa and the opportunity to socialize with a few people.

Business was good in those days. As the war started, everyone and everything seemed to be on the move. Big crops of wheat and other grains spelled good times for farmers.

In the spring of 1915, the war began to escalate and summer militia camps became active service centres with "cities" of tents in many locations. Mr. Henry Lawson, son of the agent at Dominion City, asked superiors to transfer me temporarily to an express agent position at Camp Sewell (now Camp Hughes). I supervised three or four assistants who handled express freight for the ten thousand men based at that camp. Truckloads and carloads of express moved in and out of that sta-

41

tion in 1915. We were in close contact with soldiers living in the acres of tents.

Mr. Lawson made nine per cent on all express shipment. Out of these commissions, he paid me seventy-five dollars and the assistants a total of one hundred dollars — and there was still a lot left over.

We lived in work cars featuring beds and tables and ate in the dining car, where Joe the cook looked after us very well. Our dessert each night was CPR strawberries — in other words, prunes.

When the camp closed for winter, I received a call from the chief. He informed me that I was the successful applicant for the position of day operator at Emerson. This town on the Canada-United States border was only ten miles (or sixteen kilometres) from Dominion City. That seemed like the luckiest day of my life. I couldn't get there fast enough. Finally, I had a permanent position that paid well and was close to home.

The Emerson posting was a challenging position. It required skills, specifically the Morse code operations that had been my first love. Now, typing aptitude really came into play and I studied hard and went to work with pleasure. Even walking to work on extremely cold winter mornings failed to dampen my enthusiasm for the sound of the telegraph instrument.

However, the news coming over those wires was grim. The list of Canadian casualties grew longer and recruiting became more intense. The army formed companies of soldiers from smaller towns, who went overseas together. When I was approached to join the Royal Canadian Signals, I accepted willingly. The CPR, a deeply patriotic company which encouraged its employees to enlist, assured me that I would not lose my seniority and would return to my same position. They also gave all volunteers six months pay, to be distributed monthly. I assigned mine to my mother.

My decision saddened Mother, Dad and Grannie but they were extremely patriotic. They had seen the boys from our town going off and read the casualty lists in the newspaper. They knew that more sol-

diers were needed. They agreed that I could do no less for Canada and our close ally, Great Britain.

Will was at the University of Manitoba but he enlisted and would head overseas shortly after me. Both of us would be in the communications branch of the Canadian Army and serve close by one another.

My life — and my attitude — were about to undergo profound changes.

CARRY ON

4

A New Attitude

World War I affected my whole life. It educated my body and soul — my being, my attitude, my outlook, my drive. You got used to practically everything in the army and quickly forgot, but each experience lived with you forever.

The sight of dead men after a battle was sickening. The first "War to End All Wars" was long ago but, upon reflection, the stench and bloodshed rush back.

Above all, that war made me very thankful. Even today, I can't show my gratitude sufficiently. To think that I escaped all the bombardments and raids . . . I rarely talk about my war experiences because I don't think people would believe me, simply because they weren't there. Now, I realize that you have to be courageous as well to overcome war's memories. Certain incidents still haunt me, but I think I've overcome them enough to tell you about them and forget them again — for a while.

In the spring of 1916, I left my railway job in Emerson and returned to Dominion City to bid my family farewell. I spent the night at home with Mother, Dad, Grannie, Will — still at home looking after the farm, Wallace, who was working in a bank, Helen and our friends. We knelt together in prayer and asked God to ensure the Allies a victory — and my safe return. It was a very touching and emotional scene. I'll never forget that day because I heard my mother say: "You're leaving now my tender care, Remember child, your mother's prayer." That is a saying I continue to repeat often.

The scene was reminiscent of our childhood. Every morning after breakfast we got down on our knees and said our prayers. Each night, we knelt at our mother's feet. As I prepared to depart, there was a lot of weeping, but I was excited and anxious to get overseas before the war ended.

The train from Emerson to Winnipeg left at six o'clock in the morning. A lot of friends from the town came to the train station to say goodbye: church and civic leaders, all the CPR staff. I was quite sad to leave my loved ones but my patriotism saw me through my departure.

Two other men and I pulled away from the platform on the train that was so familiar to me. We never thought the war would last. We figured it would be over in a year or so.

I went to Minto Barracks in Winnipeg and enlisted with the Royal Canadian Mechanical Engineers. Until the Battle of Vimy Ridge, the whole Canadian Army was under the British Army.

Our orders sent us immediately to Lansdowne Park in Ottawa for special training. Former civilian telegraphers, operators, train dispatchers and professional press telegraphers were grouped together to learn the Continental Code. We quickly learned the eight symbols, all numerals, with buzzers instead of sounders, and were posted overseas to replace those who died in the terrible battle at Mons.

Our unit, which consisted entirely of telegraphers, was to become part of the newly created Fifth Division within the Canadian Corps. We left from Halifax on a ship called the Baltic.

The trip was traumatic, but not merely because we were heading to the battlefields. Four years earlier, on the night of April 14-15, 1912, the Titanic had struck an iceberg and sunk in the north Atlantic. According to the book, Titanic, by Leo Marriott, no fewer than 1,522 people perished that out of a total of 2,235 passengers and crew. The public outcry was tremendous. It ended so tragically that the whole world was shocked. News of the disaster flashed on the telegraph and splashed across the front page of the Winnipeg Free Press. The unthinkable had happened. It was very early in wireless days. In fact,

the Titanic's crew use of wireless communication helped determine its location. Press reports had claimed that the ship was designed not to sink under any circumstances and it was unbelievable to think so many people died so unnecessarily.

Travelling the ocean to go to war. I couldn't help but think about the disaster. It was an unheard of possibility and here we were attempting to cross the same ocean. How much more vulnerable we were, two thousand troops escorted by a British cruiser called the Drake. She saw us through the whole passage. It was very emotional. We zig-zagged across the water, avoiding territory where submarines might be expected. We thought we could sink just like the Titanic. She stayed in our hearts a long time — and still does.

We went overseas strictly out of patriotism. Our pride in our country was compelling. Nobody in the unit I was in was conscripted. (Conscription was what Americans know as the draft.) I wouldn't have been conscripted because I was classified as an essential worker in Canada, but we were needed overseas. We weren't professional soldiers but we never wavered from the philosophy that we had to serve where we could serve the best, wherever we might be needed.

An awful lot of CPR employees went — train dispatchers, telegraphers, officers, track men and so on. The increasing nationalism flowed like a river that just kept getting stronger. Officers taught us we were fighting for freedom. It wasn't a sense of power but, rather, a sense of the cause, namely the continuation of a democratic world.

There were no financial rewards. I was paid one dollar and ten cents per day, half of which I assigned to my mother — and that was it. My ability to communicate by various methods earned me a preferred posting to the Corps headquarters, from which I operated with all units of the Canadian forces. There were about twelve or fifteen in our wireless communications group.

Upon arrival in England, we were required to undergo rigorous infantry training with rifle, bayonet and gas mask because you never knew when you were going to be called on. Two or three times per

week, we went on marches, real tough marches, for ten or twelve miles.

Now we knew what being in the army was all about. Right from the start, you lost your identity. As the deaths mounted, soldiers and entire troops struggled to maintain their character. For instance, in the Fifth Division, we had purple patches on the shoulders of our uniforms but, as the division was dismantled and various units were sent to the battlegrounds, these purple patches were replaced by the insignias of the units in which we served. You were trained to be an individual soldier and use your own intelligence in any emergency. We became known by our regimental numbers. Mine was 504131.

You were under complete control of the army. We were subject to the will of the military — every day. Permission had to be granted for everything that you did. You were trained to do things individually but you were still under the command. I got to the point where I accepted discipline, especially self-discipline, and enjoyed it. This self-discipline would register in my mind forever. I made myself happy in every circumstance but I didn't feel like a free person in the army. I felt like I was completely dominated. As a soldier, you were part of the army, subject to all the senior officers' wishes. They tried to keep your attitude firm. I always thought they were trying to break my spirit but they didn't have much success.

Senior officers prescribed intense pre-battle training, which kept us active and fit. You had to be in good shape. They'd walk you and run you, and if you weren't able to complete the drills, you had to go to the doctor. While we awaited our postings, we were organized into groups for games which became part of our training. I played on the Signal Corps soccer and lacrosse teams.

We carried our armour all the time. In our enlistment papers, it said that we could be called into the place where we were needed most. Every man was taught to fill in wherever needed. The rules were the same for all sappers, as we were called. Even the cooks had to take that training. (Army training taught me some real lessons because all through life, I felt that I was exempt from nothing.) We were thor-

48

oughly trained in infantry training and ready for battle.

To appease our strong hunger, we ate a lot of "Bully" beef, soup and bread with butter and jam and drank tea. The Salvation Army Hut had a tea cauldron any time we came off duty. We would always go there because we were assured of a cup of tea. They had canteens and a lot of stuff there. We all had cookhouse routine and guard routine, too.

And then there were the latrines. If you had to use the toilet, we had pretty well permanent latrines, mostly above ground, and you headed to them. They were very sanitary. (Sanitary means acceptable.) We all pulled some duty on the "honey wagon" detail. I had to clean out the wooden boxes underneath the toilets. You just did it because it had to be done.

The mess tables had to be clean. So did your uniform. It didn't matter whether your shoes were dirty or not. You had to shine them anyway. Spit and polish. You'd go for a shower, always outdoors, two or three times a week, if you were lucky. We even had to parade to the showers occasionally.

It was great training. It stayed with me all my life. You had to keep your bunk clean because it was inspected every day in the barracks and on the battlefield. Fortunately, I was a specially trained communications man and managed to avoid some — but not all — of the most degrading duties.

Our training continued for about a year and a half in Great Britain, between 1916 and early 1918, as we waited anxiously for orders, hopefully, to head to the front in France.

Still, we thought we weren't doing enough, because we were far away from the front line. "What are you going to tell your grandchildren about the war?" we'd ask each other. The reply was always the same. "S.F.A." In other words, sweet fuck all. You thought you weren't rewarded. Maybe it was an expression of disappointment. "What did you do in the Great War?" we imagined ourselves being asked. "S.F.A.," came the reply. "What did you do today?" "S.F.A."

When the wireless came out, we were so busy with classes because

it was something new. We were preparing for open warfare and we always had to transmit info. Until now, ground communication was about all we could use because the telephone lines, still relatively new technology, were broken up. You might say the wireless was a last resort to communication in battle. We had the equipment all the time but it wasn't used, as far as I know, until we went to France. The code was the same as the one used in telegraphy but the operation of the wireless itself didn't

DIRT ROAD DISPATCHER: As part of my training, I couriered dispatches between corps headquarters in Kent and general headquarters in London. Spear Family Photo

require any wire, except a ground aerial. You could send through the ground or through the air. The ground transmission was sent with a heavy spark. There was a spark with the air transmission too but it wasn't that heavy.

Our wireless unit was also trained in all aspects of signalling: the telegraph, flagging, night light, and heliograph which used the sun. We moved frequently and unpredictably across Great Britain. I think I was likely the youngest member of our unit. Some of these clever wireless experts were in their mid-to-late thirties but they treated me with

50

respect because of my ability to handle the wire services as well as the best of them.

The signal corps had dispatch riders and dispatch runners. I, like everyone else in our unit, took a regular shift as a dispatch messenger, riding a motorbike across dirt roads from our corps headquarters around Kent to general headquarters in London. The bike had a single cylinder and you had to push it a bit to get around shell holes.

There was heavy wartime traffic going to and from ports. Dispatch riders rode motorcycles. We used bicycles on leaves to London, known as "the Big Smoke" and other parts of England that most of us had heard about growing up in Canada but never actually seen.

We in the wireless unit were specially trained men. Officers had to keep us on duty. Keeping you healthy was the number one concern. Your body was a piece of machinery — part of the big show, part of the monster of war — and you had to keep it going. Senior officers stressed how much money they had invested in us. It was hard to think that way but they instilled the belief that we were valuable commodities.

"Fall out the sick!" a commander would say during inspections. You stepped forward and marched off to the doctor. Nothing was private. You got used to this way of thinking and didn't think anything of it because you did what you were told to do. It was part of the deal. You signed your life away. If you didn't fit into one place, they just posted you somewhere else. Everything was done without your consent. All you had was a duffel bag, shoulder bag and backpack. Your duffel bag, known as your kit bag, contained socks, underwear and maybe (if you were lucky) a spare pair of shoes and a waterproof ground sheet that you could drape over your shoulders as a cape or sleep on. If you didn't have a ground sheet to cover you, you just had a cap with a wire rim in it. You had to carry your water bottle and keep it filled. You had emergency rations — a can of bully beef and a bag of hard biscuits that resembled salad croutons. This survival kit would sustain you. If you didn't have those emergency rations, you were charged. You were punished with extra cleaning duties.

On duty and sometimes in training, I had to have my gas mask available for easy use. As part of standard orders, I carried my rifle everywhere and slept right beside it at night. Officers called arms inspections at any time and your gun had to be pretty clean, boy. They gave you a pull-through and all the equipment you needed to keep your barrel in good shape. I kept mine clean all the time but once, in France, a guy sleeping in the next bunk took my rifle and left me his dirty gun. I got three days "C.B." — confined to barracks — for that infraction.

I complained about the switch. The guy said he didn't do it on purpose but I knew he didn't keep his rifle clean. He brought mine back but the damage was done. Officers deemed me guilty.

We were allowed to get a clean pair of underwear from time to time. You picked up a clean set as you turned your dirty set in. Often, you had to remove bed bugs from the underwear. They were dead but they were stuck in it. You didn't make a big fuss about that because it was just normal procedure.

Living among men for so long, sex became the chief topic of conversation during leave but, before you went and after you came back, you had to go on a "short arm" parade. It was a humiliating experience. "Short arm" was the nickname for your penis. We lined up outside the doctor's door and, when the doctor shouted "Next!" we marched one by one into his office. He would pull back your foreskin and examine it for signs of venereal disease. He would give you condoms, whether or not you wanted them, and a stern warning. "Don't think you can go out and screw everybody in the world and get away with it," one told me. If you came back with V.D. your name was posted on a bulletin board and you lost your daily pay of one dollar and ten cents. "It's a crime," doctors warned. The army kept the cases hush hush, but most soldiers had a good idea of who was sick. (I knew guys that came home with syphilis and gonorrhea and the diseases changed their lives forever. Disgrace was the word. Humiliation.)

In London and Brussels, there were actually wax figures of men and women who had contracted venereal disease. They depicted the effects

of syphilis, gonor-
rhea and other dis-
eases, illustrating
how they affect
your body. These
visual pictures, the
army's way of bat-
tling promiscuous
behaviour among
the troops, were
just frightening —
like ruination. You
felt that your body
would be contami-
nated for life. You
tried so hard to build it up and you yourself wanted to be clean.

BEST BUDDIES: *From left to right are Terry Kidd, Harold Elliott, myself, and Tracy Kew. I guess Kew was thinking it was bed time.* Spear Family Photo

I considered this goal an extremely personal challenge because, before I left Dominion City, I promised my father that I would stay clean. In other words, I would keep my virginity. We had discussed potential encounters with prostitutes and the risks involved. (In Germany, they had brothels and guys that visited them told me they were very clean. That's better than communicating with people on the street, I suppose.) I didn't turn a blind eye to the so called scarlet ladies but I tried to avoid them. Oh, I still went dancing but I strived to social-ize with companions who thought the same thoughts I had, lived the same kind of a life I did, and came from a good home.

When I eventually did return to Canada, the first thing I told my dad was: "You know, I did what you told me to do. I stayed clean." His reply? "Well done."

We tried to spend our leaves in the places we had read and heard so much about — castles, churches, the Hippodrome, Albert Hall, the zoo, and amusement arenas.

Life went on as usual for the loyal Brits who welcomed us and tend-

ed to our needs. In both England and France, many soldiers' shelters, such as the Beaver Hut, Salvation Army huts, Roman Catholic huts (even though I was a Presbyterian), gave us food and lodging at minimum prices. For example, a cot and breakfast was one shilling, then equivalent to twenty-five cents Canadian.

In the spring of 1916, on one of my first leaves while still training in England, I visited Christine Ross, one of my mother's childhood friends. Married to a high-ranking London civic employee, she had corresponded with my mother for years. When Christine learned that Mother had two sons serving in Great Britain, she invited me to spend a few days at her large home.

Little did I know that I was in for a big surprise. When I arrived, my brother, Will, was there. A sapper in the Royal Canadian Engineers' section of the Canadian Signal Corps, the same corps within which I served, Will had just come over from Canada. You can imagine our joy in being reunited — best friends and brothers, far from home. Mrs. Ross immediately became known as "Mother Chrissie."

Will and I ventured all over London together but he was quickly posted to France and I followed in the summer. That London reunion, and return visits to Christine's home, set the stage for future meetings in bunkers on the French battlefield.

Other entertainment on leave came during air raids. I witnessed two in England in 1916 and 1917. They were very well organized. People would go into the underground railway stations. I saw a Zeppelin shot down over London one time. It was just a blazing mass. There was jubilation in the streets — everybody cheered. We received a little preference to get up on the rooftops and see this thing.

Hyde Park was known for having anti- aircraft guns. It was just a mass of guns. It was just the height of danger and excitement for the civilian population.

Such events just intensified our nationalism. Your sense of duty was so strong that it became demanding. Cowardice was just eliminated. You had to advance. You had to go onward and onward. The first fear

of punishment for cowardice was to be tied to a tree or something in a place where you'd be in the line of fire. I heard of that happening to people. Legend was you could be shot by your own officers. It was treated as a threat. These incidents may never have happened but we heard names of some soldiers. Such disciplinary action was considered very rare because of our strong patriotism. We told ourselves: "There's not to reason why. There's but to do or die." By the way, that line is from the Charge of the Light Brigade.

POST-PARADE: Eddie Pratt, right, of Toronto and I show off our uniforms after a parade drill at Witley Camp in Kent, England early in 1918. Spear Family Photo

I had nothing against the German people. I wanted to defeat their leaders.

Everyone in our unit knew everyone else pretty well. We came from the railway and the telegraph offices. We were a very closely united group. It was almost a family affair. Identification was almost unnecessary because you knew virtually everyone by sight.

BEHIND THE FRONT: Members of our wireless unit relax during a break in France in 1918. Such moments were precious as we placed our lives on the line every day.
Spear Family Photo

It was always the other guy that was going to get hurt. You just had to continue. I think we were all pretty well prepared to accept what came. We didn't have any say about it anyway.

That was supposed to be the war to end all wars. We were proud of the fact that Canadians had done such a good job. We wanted to get the job done. We were just absolutely dedicated to doing the work we were trained to do. There was no talk of losing. If we didn't fight, somebody else would. I never saw, or heard of any, Canadian not wanting to go to the front. Many of us were afraid it was going to be over before we got there.

When I did get there, early in 1918, it didn't take me very long to protect myself. Wireless operators were on the move all the time. We weren't equipped with artillery. We were always supported by artillery. We weren't in the front line of advance but we followed it very closely. We took grave risks.

The stretcher bearers and medical people were the same as we were. They went wherever they were required. In my breast pocket, right next to my paybook, I carried a small Bible. I read it every day and I honoured it. The verses gave me a lot of confidence and security — and,

believe me, I needed both.

Communication was the number one priority. Shifts on duty would be about eight hours but they were broken up into about two hours on and two hours off. Two or three hours at the wire was enough for one time because the cable traffic was extremely heavy. It was absolutely around the clock. You might be on the sending side or you might be on the receiving side. You would rotate.

We copied everything we heard, including German messages, in code. We didn't know what the communiques said but we had runners to get them back to headquarters for decoding. The Germans had the same methods of getting our messages too. It was just a question of decoding.

We were trained to code everything that we sent. It would be five symbols or numerals to a word. Each message indicated how many words were in the message and what priority it had. We were chosen not so much for our speed but for our accuracy.

The Germans — or Fritz as we called "him" — seemed to be able to zero in on your signals if you sent signals. If you were on the receiving end, you were quiet but, if you were sending, they would pick you up very quickly.

I became a different person in war. All the good things in life were gone, terminated very quickly. You weren't happy. You always had something to gripe about. We complained about the food, duties we perceived to be unnecessary and anything else we could think of. We asked ourselves: What was the sense of all this killing? Just for this little piece of crap?

I can remember one time when we were just going to a placement. There were quite a few pup tents. Troops had to sleep in them. I got in one of those and I thought I was safe as hell. They recommended that you lie down and take cover of some kind if there was no foxhole. At those times you sought shelter, you'd think of home. I'd ask myself, 'What are you doing here?' You wished you were somewhere else. You had no protection whatsoever. Living was just day to day and hour to

hour. All you could do was rely on yourself and get a place to dig in. (In later times, because of those experiences, I thought I could take anything.)

Many days — and every day I was in the field of fire — I didn't know whether I was going to live or die. The Germans' light artillery shells known as "whiz bangs" were especially frightening. You would hear "whiz" and then "bang." They had four-inch shell casings. Life became unpredictable. Return to the real world became unpredictable.

Instead of "hello" and "goodbye" we often said, "San Ferry Am." That was a connotation we all used. It was the soldier's farewell. It was kind of crude. We understood the meaning to be: Goodbye and screw you. It was affectionate in its own way.

We got into the mood of, 'Well, if you buy it, you've bought it.' We were really just praying. We were very much aware that many of us weren't going to make it. You'd go out with an attitude telling yourself not to lose your composure.

In the wireless section, we followed the front line advance. We were reporting the advances and positions. We sent from old barns or old shacks, whatever we could get. We intercepted all of the German wireless transmissions. It was a job. You had to be prepared to move quickly. Big guns could strike at any time. You had to stay covered, but you had to make your own cover unless you were properly situated. We usually tried to get into trenches, located just below ground level. We got bombed out of trenches by a lot of shelling and aircraft bombing which, unlike in England, I certainly did not find entertaining.

The aircraft bombing was the worst. I saw quite a few aircraft go down, particularly when the Germans were fighting and trying to knock out our observation balloons. I saw a German plane take four Allied balloons out one after the other, about half a mile apart or so. They just went up in smoke. The crews ejected from the baskets underneath and came down in parachutes. Often crews stuck to their balloons as long as they could and tried to fight off the Germans. We had fighter planes stationed very close to the balloons. If enemy aircraft got

close enough to shoot the balloons down, the pilots knew they had to get the hell out, because there was nothing they could do. The balloons had machine guns but they were very ineffective at that time.

During an air raid, you headed for cover immediately. You would hear the machine gun rattle but you mostly heard the exploding shells. You didn't know where they were going to go because you couldn't hear them before they hit the ground. We were pretty well protected during the daytime but, at night, you could hardly trace where they were going. The Germans would do anything they could to frighten you. They were after the ammunition dumps.

You'd only know what was going on in front of you. You were only one small part of your territory. After an air raid, you were very anxious to get up and see what was going on. We were privy to a lot of communications that would give the exact places where they would bomb. We were pretty sure they were trying to defend against us rather than advance. I don't think they had the reserves to make an advance, although they caught the Americans, who fought beside us, a couple of times. You never knew when they were coming out of the sky. You continuously had to go underground. There were lots of places to go. You had your wireless equipment, which resembled a telegraph, that you had to take with you.

When the shells came in, they sounded terrifying. I was so damned scared. You didn't run away. You just ran for cover. My thoughts were simply to get down. You jumped into the first dugout you could find. The dugouts, or bunkers, were set up deep underground. We tried to get above ground for meals but we lived underground.

It was safe territory. Under the circumstances, we were as safe as safe could be. There were sleeping quarters down there. We slept mostly on wire cots, two or three high. They were comfortable. Some of them had a layer of straw on them.

If there wasn't any heavy shelling, we slept in broken-down buildings or were billeted. Sometimes we slept in tents but they were easy to observe, so often we crawled into cellars and other hideaways. The

dugouts were dusty and trampled down because they had been used before. It just depended what kind of a front you were on. They were livable.

Rats also resided in the dugouts. We didn't seem to mind the rats but we couldn't leave the food unprotected.

The wireless people also had to go out to observations posts in groups of three to six. That was just for interception of German code.

We didn't have very long shifts. We worked a maximum of two hours. We got a lot of rest but it was pretty scary stuff. You would really bare your feelings to your mates. I was indebted to a lot of comrades in war time. They gave me tremendous support. I would remain friends with them for many decades afterward. What you said just depended how close the shells would come to you. We tried to make a joke of the horror. We tried to put a face on it.

We thought we were pretty darn lucky to be doing the communications work. We told ourselves we could have been in a lot worse places. You had to pull yourself up by your bootstraps and say, 'I'm going to get out of it.' You really had to like yourself.

On our way back from the front, we saw many of the wounded at field dressing stations. They would transport the wounded by light rail or ambulance to ships that took them back to Britain. They were the homes of the medical units, the ambulance corps.

The medics did a great job. The field dressing stations consisted of big, camouflaged tents. To me, they were places of horror. You would see soldiers with amputated legs and arms. Bodies were piled up like cordwood. I was on one burying party — that was enough. It was a required exercise. Every soldier had two dogtags for identification, one red and one green. At the field dressing stations, we took the red dog tag — the symbol of death — from dead soldiers. A lot of information was on that tag so we sent it back to headquarters. That was how casualty records were kept. We had to get as many dog tags as we could.

I felt extremely lucky and just wanted to get out of that duty as soon as I could. On one occasion, we buried several German soldiers. They

had identification tags too. The bodies had already been laid out and we put them in their graves.

This burial party is something I try to forget. I never talk about it — never — because it was too weird. At the time I thought, "You have to do a job. Do it." That was when you realized how fortunate you were. You wouldn't think that civilized people could continue viewing these scenes. It was gruesome. Even to see the Germans lying out there was hard. You always had to think, "Well, somebody loves you." Cleanup was a hell of a job. Sidearms and that sort of thing were left on. Some soldiers would pick them up and try to keep them as souvenirs, although I couldn't bring myself to do that.

I wouldn't want anybody to see the field dressing stations or battle-ground after an advance. You had to steel yourself to see it. You had to get yourself into a state where you felt "This is the gory side of war" — because that's what it was.

The first ten days after the big push that started August 8, 1918, I could take you to a trench that had been taken by tanks and you'd have seen dead German soldiers lined up on the banks of that trench cooking in the sun. That was bad. After all, they were human beings. There is a little humanity in everybody.

That's something I never told anybody about the war. The stench was unbearable. You tried to keep going and forget the deaths. You were on the move and that was it. There was a purpose and we weren't going to deter from it. You were there for yourself and for your mates. You had a very strong resolve to control yourself. You could not show cowardice. That was very humiliating. I don't know if I showed my bravery very well or not.

Guys would get what was known as S.I.F., a self-inflicted wound. Soldiers found guilty of that were subject to court-martial. You'd hear about so and so and so and so, who shot themselves in the foot to get out of battle. That's how expression shooting yourself in the foot, which is even used today, came about. The connotation was that, if you took yourself out of battle, you were considered a coward. (I never

knew of anyone who did that.)

We also heard about young men who were hospitalized because they broke down mentally and were unable to return to battle. These stories hardened my resolve to be mentally tough. I strived to display my bravery at all times. So did my brother, Will. We visited each other on the battlefield as frequently as we could. There were no telephones, so we had to communicate through the grapevine. We had access to each other's command. Other soldiers knew that we were brothers and let each of us know where the other was. We managed to see each other about every two weeks. If we were on rest, we'd walk overland, say a mile, behind the line. We jumped into bunkers or dugouts and shared our experiences. We always talked about the same thing, our experiences at home and the latest word we had from home. We received packages and letters from our parents, grandmother, and friends. During those visits, we recalled our school days in Manitoba and made a pact that the survivor would go home and tell our parents not to grieve. (This pact made a strong man of me, dedicated to the protection of family. I came to believe that a person must have two or three priorities and the first was my country — before everything.)

We were always within range of enemy guns but there might be no occasion for Fritzy to shell a place if there wasn't some kind of attack or raid. We thought we were relatively safe. We went to a place called Caines on July 1, 1918, for a sports day. The whole Canadian Corps competed. Will was there but we didn't spend much time together because we each had our own thing to do. We were ten or twenty miles away from the front.

I already knew at that time there was going to be a big push. At the end of the day, our wireless unit was heading back to the barracks when, suddenly, we heard the screech of a German shell coming our way. It certainly woke everybody up. We scattered and ran for cover. The shell didn't hit anyone. We believed it was just Fritzy sending us a little message. It was just a taste of what was to come.

As weapons and technology became more sophisticated, we were

shifting away from static warfare, when we fired at each other mostly from the trenches and there was very little movement. At first we were defending, straightening out the line in places, and waiting to find out who was opposed and who was another. Now, in 1918, we were in a different phase — of open warfare.

The Germans had an impregnable line fortified by cement dugouts known as pillboxes, which had apertures for the machine gun nozzles on the defending side. The only way you could take them was with a direct hit. The infantry and cavalry couldn't take them. They were so formidable that they had to be destroyed by gunfire.

The Canal du Nord was the strongest point on the German line. We could never take it without intense bombardment. The high command didn't reveal much to the troops but, since I was in communications, I had a little bit of early knowledge. I learned we were really going to give it to Fritz. Through the communications I sent and received, I knew very well that we were planning to break through. Will and I were particularly aware that there was going to be one big "show" as we called it. We knew there was going to be a big try for a breakthrough, similar to the creeping barrage method at Vimy Ridge.

We started to bring our heavy equipment up and hide it under camouflage in the woods. Heavy artillery and guns were being assembled close behind the front line near Arras. We were pretty sure we were going to get into a situation with all the guns coming up and all the tanks moving. We had always, more or less, known that we were going to have to invade Germany because we had trained for that.

Senior officers later confirmed our hunches. We were on call day and night. Everybody was told what they had to do. Each man, to the lowest rank, knew his responsibilities. Everybody was pretty well of the same mind. They wanted to be in on the big push. Nobody was going to stop us. It was planned on the strength of advanced training and firepower. When the breakthrough occurred, the troops would leapfrog up the countryside. Possibly, the Germans suspected something but they didn't know when the attack would occur. Surprise was key and the

secret was well kept.

Realizing the magnitude of the battle, I wanted to see Will. This was just before August 8 and we were pretty close to the jumping off phase. I was assigned to a dugout for observation and he just happened to be close. I knew where the headquarters were and I had about six hours off. Will was maintaining a guard post in the cellar of a bombed-out building in a courtyard at Arras, very close to Third Brigade headquarters. My armbands signalled that I could go anywhere but I still felt I was taking a chance. I felt I was heading to a place where I really wasn't supposed to be — but I was determined to see my brother.

When I got there, the cavalry had just come in on horseback. I had never seen horses in France before. The Canal du Nord was up ahead a little bit, maybe a half a mile. That was the front line.

It was lovely weather. Will introduced me to the guys around his section and we renewed our pledge to tell our parents not to grieve for us if one of us didn't make it back. We figured it wouldn't be too long before the war was over. We were pretty sure that this was the beginning of the end. We were quite jubilant and optimistic. We thought we were in comparative safety.

Suddenly, shells began exploding all around us. There was just a barrage of light artillery fire. I thought, "Something is happening. I better get the hell out of here." I was also due back on duty soon. Will was also due back on duty and he had to go.

"Now, you be careful," he said. Before I left he said: "Drop me a line. I want to tell you something." I think he was going to tell me that he had become engaged but, as the shell fire continued, he couldn't leave his post. It was the last time I saw him.

I had a hell of a time getting out of there, as I dodged the German quick-firing light artillery. Somehow, I got to the courtyard. There were all these horses tethered in the yard. Time was irrelevant. Survival was of the essence. I never saw the shrapnel when it hit me in the left wrist. It was just a bursting shell. It was skinny gut shrapnel. I didn't know I'd been hit until blood started trickling down through my glove.

I vaguely recall running under the frantic horses' bellies as they tried to free themselves. It was just a bloody mess. It was a slaughter. I couldn't tell you how long the onslaught lasted. (I've tried to visualize myself back there but my mind just becomes blank.) I think everything happened in less than half an hour. I couldn't even tell you what success they had with the barrage, except that they got into the horses.

I felt terrible after I was wounded. Perhaps I shouldn't have been in that place because, remember, I wasn't on duty at the time. I didn't want to be taken out because I was one of very few trained for wireless communications, so I never went to a field dressing station. A medic bandaged me up and inoculated me. The wound was superficial, although my left wrist still bears a scar. I never reported the injury.

When we started to advance on Aug. 8, it was different work altogether. You had to move everything with you and also you had to prepare for counter attack. We started our attack with big nine-inch guns firing from the rear, three hundred or four hundred yards behind our positions, for three or four miles along the Canadian front, and a good many miles on either side. Our artillery blazed out with everything that could be fired. We surprised our enemies and advanced at incredible speed through their wire entrenchments.

Open warfare was about to reach its peak. Canadian and Australian troops launched the attack at Amiens, aiming to push the Germans back to Germany and force them to surrender. Our Canadian Corps advanced almost thirteen kilometres (eight miles) that day and, as historian Ken MacLeod noted in Canada and World War I, it "was one of the deepest penetrations made in a single day during the war."

At the same time, I was transferred to a wireless communications truck and on duty around the clock. The truck reported advancements and intercepted German messages. That wireless truck was pretty posh, I'll tell you. It was a pretty big truck too and had solid rubber tires. It was something very new. I think there was only that one truck in the whole Canadian corps. We used it to very good advantage.

Still, we were subject to shell fire, aircraft and all kinds of gunnery.

There were certain places that you just couldn't get through because they were so badly bombarded.

Neville St. Vaast was a terrible place. There were four roads there and the Germans had them pinpointed. If they saw any kind of movement from their observation posts, they just blasted. We had to try to do everything at night. Even then, they still had the range. That was just pure hell to get through. It was a very scary place.

All through August and September, our Canadian and other Allied forces made spectacular advances and took thousands of prisoners to our wire cages behind the lines. Many of those prisoners were just school kids of seventeen or eighteen. I thought I was young at twenty but those so called soldiers were just cadets.

We treated them well. They knew that the war was over for them and they were much better fed than when they were fighting, so they gave us little trouble. This is not to discount their predicament because it could quite easily have been the other way around — with us being the prisoners.

By now, the advancing troops had reached the heavily fortified positions of the enemy pill boxes defended by machine guns. We achieved this territory in the terrible Battle of Amiens, where the top command threw everyone into battle at the front — against intolerable odds. I heard, through the grapevine, that Will was injured in the onslaught. I thought, "Well, you lucky guy. You'll be back in England by now," because medical crews moved the injured out very quickly. I looked forward to seeing him again soon because the word was out that the war was about to end.

Meanwhile, our wireless truck advanced rapidly towards Valencinnes in Belgium. The Germans had rearguards but our troops were getting to them. They had to give up because we were overwhelmingly powerful. The message we had all been awaiting anxiously came through at 7:10 a.m. on November, 11, 1918. I was on duty in a telegraph office. We had a receiver and a sender. I was on the sender and Bill Collins of what was then known as Berlin, Ont. — it's now

known as Kitchener — was on the receiver. "Hostilities will cease at 1100 hours Nov. 11. Troops will stand fast on the line reached at that hour which will be reported to army headquarters. Defensive precautions will be maintained. There will be no intercourse with enemy."

Well, the bloodshed continued right up until eleven o'clock that day — and some lives were lost — but the war did, in fact, end. We were going home.

I was immediately assigned to Canadian Corps headquarters and

BRAVE BROTHER: I show this photo of Will in his army uniform to family and friends as a way of honouring his memory. But thinking of his death still evokes sadness. Spear Family Photo

ordered to go to Mons. The Armistice was signed on November 11th at eleven o'clock in the morning at Compiegne.

Being in Valenciennes at the time, I had a firsthand view of the German motorcade arriving in all its plumage and splendor to surrender to the Canadian Corps. I'll never forget that parade as long as I live. They came right to our headquarters, in limousines and on horseback. They wore the traditional brilliantly colored German uniforms, with spikes on their helmets. You would never know they had lost the war. The Germans appeared the conquerors rather than the vanquished. How proud they appeared to us. I imagined that similar scenes were playing out all across the French countryside. I thought to myself, "By

God, that could have been us surrendering."

However, while most were jubilant, there was little happiness within me. I was extremely sad because I had received a report through the grapevine that Will had died of his wounds. I later learned in a letter from the Red Cross: "Spt. Spear's was badly wounded by hostile machine gun bullets on the 27th September in the left shoulder. He was doing work as forward lineman and up to the time of his being wounded, his conduct was so exemplary that he had been awarded the Military Medal.

"The N.C.O. in charge of the party had his wounds dressed and had him carried to a Field Ambulance but he died on the way . . . "

He was twenty-three years old. That same day, September 27th, proved to be an historic day for Canada as our forces breached the Hindenburg Line, taking such German strongholds as Canal du Nord, the Marquion Line, and Bourlon Wood, but it was bitter to hear that Will's company had stood no chance at all, that so many perished in that awful fight at Canal du Nord. All were very young men, between the ages of nineteen and twenty-two — all Canadians who died in the name of freedom. They were among an estimated 45,000 Canadian casualties between August 8th and November 11th.

I felt terrible that Will had died so close to the end of the war. The grapevine was accurate. (I still have my brother's dog tag — No. 506319 — although the red colour has faded. I also have my own green dog tag, which symbolizes survival.)

Still, I told myself the rejoicing because the war was over was the important thing. It was a joyous occasion for the Belgian people, who had been occupied and known no freedom for five or six long years, so I struggled to celebrate with them.

I was chosen to go to Bonn with the Army of Occupation. I went to Mons, the site of the official German surrender, as our troops organized for the trek. I came upon our old friend, Cyril Wallace, the boy (now a man) who had been saved by Will at the swimming hole during younger, happier years. He was on his way back to civilian life in

London.

"Where is Will?" he asked after greeting me with a hug. When he heard the sad news, he fell to the street with shock and grief. I was grieving so badly about Bill, as I had often called him. I just wanted to go home, but first I had to go to Bonn.

From Mons, we started our journey on foot and traversed through Belgium, passing through such towns as Schleider and Liege. This was a different world, indeed. We moved in daylight with no bombing, no artillery shells, and no enemy aircraft to scare us. Peace had come again.

At Bonn, we took up our positions of defence, as if still at war, and continued in communications and guard duty throughout the winter. The German people were tired of war, had many hardships to endure, and their food was scarce. However, they were very civil to our soldiers. We had strict orders that there be "no intercourse with the enemy." Some Canadian troops destroyed the German kaiser's statue in Bonn's town square, but they were quickly court-martialled. Senior officers wouldn't stand for that. They thought that was a sign of disrespect to the German people.

As the occupation continued into the spring of 1919, my chum, Bob Henderson, and I wanted to get leave to go to Ireland. He was stationed just across the Rhine River from our headquarters and he was able to get the same date for departure that I had obtained. We were to meet in London on March 8th, at a railway station and stay at the station master's office to get any messages about our departure to Ireland.

I came in from Calais, France, after managing to get transportation on anything that moved to the channel ports. I had turned in my rifle and battle equipment to the stores for safekeeping and planned to return to duty two weeks hence. I fully expected to return to Bonn. I arrived at Trafalgar Station and was making my way to the depot office when I looked over on the next platform where another train had just pulled out and there was my friend, Bob.

That was a splendid meet. We were both dolled up in our best uni-

forms, badges and divisional patches on our shoulder straps. Our unit dress was cavalry breeches and tunics to match and, of course, we had to have identification colours to match our furlough passes, particularly to Ireland.

Our first stop was Dublin, where we registered at the Four Courts Hotel. This was a first class hotel, but we found that we were not very welcome on the streets. We were immediately identified as English soldiers and our presence did not sit well with the Sinn Fein, the political arm of today's Irish Republican Army, which opposes British home rule. Even then they were active and dangerous characters. We were actually booed in this city and we decided it was not safe or pleasant to be in this place.

We scrambled out of the hotel as quickly as possible, and that proved to be a fortuitous move — because they burned down the Four Courts the next day. (So trouble in Ireland isn't anything new.) From Dublin, we went to Belfast, where the locals welcomed us and made us feel comfortable. We were able to see the beautiful country and lovely city. In the YMCA, we met a medical sergeant who had a good deal going. He offered us admission to, and discharge from Belfast Military Hospital, dated two weeks in advance, for one quid. We both accepted it, taking a chance that it might not fly when we got back to the provost marshall in London, where we were required to report after our leave in Ireland. So we enjoyed another two weeks in picturesque and peaceful Belfast and saw the city from virtually every angle.

We returned to London without incident but, when we saw the provost marshall, he had some news for us. Our units had moved from Bonn and we awaiting embarkation orders from Kimmel Park in Rhyl, Wales. At last, we were going home to Canada. We had to take our turn with the boats.

There was a big clamor. The Americans were demanding to get back home. There was some riots in Ryhl. We were in a camp in Wales for disembarkation and getting lined up for the embarkation ships. There was quite a bad riot, but I was very fortunate. I got away quickly. They

were so anxious to get home. There were a lot of troops. But you had to go in your turn. We were trying to get the guys who were overseas the longest back in a reasonable time.

Of course, the Americans had come a while later than we had and we thought they were getting some privileges. There was a lot of discipline handed out for that. We were still in the army and we were subject to army law. While in Rhyl, I contacted Mrs. Rattray, a friend from Dominion City. Her husband was now Brigadier General Rattray and in charge of the huge camp of troops waiting to get on a transport ship. She wrote to me and asked me to let her know when I would be in Southampton, England, which I did. When our train pulled in, there was General Rattray's staff car, waiting to pick me up. I didn't go to the waiting camp at all because Mrs. Rattray insisted I stay with her until our unit was assigned a place on the next vessel out of port. I received the same treatment from her home to the dock. That was something to see — and experience — a sapper getting out of a brig's staff car. The general's flag didn't fly on the fender, as was customary, but it had plenty of other VIP markings.

Once on board our transport for home, I was just an ordinary soldier with no special assignment. The ship was terribly overcrowded and several members of our wireless section from Bonn were assigned the engine room hammock space. That is where I stayed for the next four days — sick, sick, sick from the smell of burning diesel fuel and the boat pitching day and night. I couldn't eat a thing, but then the seas became calmer and I was able to get out on deck.

I never will forget that feeling of freedom with no worries, in stark contrast to our trip over on the Baltic with a destroyer escort. This time, the waters were peaceful. There was no fear of submarines or torpedoes — we were just heading home. Sometime during this period, I underwent a transformation. I can't say exactly when it occurred because, after all these years, this mode of thinking has become deeply ingrained in my soul. Because of Will's death, I was feeling a little overwhelmed and not thinking things out. The very fact that I had survived was so

overwhelming. I felt that it was necessary to change my attitude. World War I had made life much more important to me. It gave me a sense of being very fortunate to survive and a strong feeling that I owed the country something for that. Despite the devastating loss of my brother, I vowed to carry on. I just felt that I was extremely fortunate to go back home a free man and developed a much deeper appreciation of my family and friends.

World War I really taught me that you have to be at peace with your neighbour. I learned that there is nothing romantic about war. I signed up because I felt I had a duty to serve my country but I quickly discovered that war is terrible and should be avoided at all costs. Also, you must be careful not to find fault, because prejudice is a terrible thing. The war showed me that the world is made up of a lot of different mentalities. If you can attain an attitude of impartiality, faith and patriotism, you can be happy. To think of the thousands who died, and the potential outstanding contributions to the world that were lost forever, was unfathomable. I realized that peace must prevail under any circumstances. Diplomacy must be our greatest weapon.

Clearly, World War I was the part of my early life that shaped the rest of it. The rules and daily supervision had just been so suffocating. When I dropped that load off my shoulders, the feeling of relief was just tremendous. I was free again. This freedom inspired me and made my life very easy. It was a very inspirational time. I experienced an awakening, a real awakening. If I hadn't changed my attitude, I wouldn't have had the serenity that I have today. I can live with anybody now. That means peace of mind, just real peace of mind.

Despite the tragedy of my brother's death, World War I was a tremendous personal experience. I returned to Canada with a very happy attitude. I just felt euphoria. There were no bombs. Everything was quiet. I felt like all the fences around me were down. I became my own boss. What was to be was up to me. I set my eye (i.e. my goals) pretty high and devoted myself to community living. I wasn't afraid to tackle anything. I had great ambitions to have a family and do my part

in every endeavour, wherever I lived.
  I knew I had reached manhood then.

Carry On

5

Starting a Family

My wonderful family's love and affection made my homecoming in Dominion City a time of great joy and, sometimes, sadness. I experienced feelings of euphoria but also powerful pangs of grief and disbelief at Will's death — but I vowed to carry on. The newspapers and older generations made a great deal about young people aged eighteen to twenty-one who died during the war and what they would miss in life. Their dreams had been destroyed in a very violent way.

Thankful that I had been spared, I yearned to enjoy a peaceful life. I was full of hope for an exciting and successful future. I reported to the superintendent of our Canadian Pacific Railway division in Winnipeg and he advised me to take as much rest time as I needed. A job as a telegraph operator in Emerson would be mine as soon as I felt comfortable with the work required. So I spent time with Dad and Wallace, who were running our sixty-acre farm. It would just be a matter of time before Wallace embarked on a prosperous career in the banking and brokerage business which would culminate as western region supervisor for James Richardson and Sons.

I also enjoyed special moments with my former tomboy sister Helen, who had transformed into a slender and pretty young woman. She was completing Grade 12 and would soon leave for Normal School in Winnipeg, where she would receive her elementary school teaching credential.

Also enjoying special times with Mother and Grannie, I took long

75

walks, ate wholesome meals, enjoyed long peaceful nights of sleep and visited friends and returning soldiers. After three and a half years under strict military conditions, life in Manitoba seemed luxurious. In the summer, I went down to Emerson to look over the situation and arranged for a place to live in a rooming house, because I knew that I wanted that CPR position. I moved in with Mr. and Mrs. Frank Haynes, who provided fine room and board to many single young ex-soldiers.

I returned to my telegraph operator's post in August of 1919. I was ready to go back and delighted to have regular hours, although five o'clock in the morning was a very early start. Mr. and Mrs. Haynes provided good meals and comfortable room for their boarders, including fellow ex-soldiers Tom Bedwell, Gordon Hulme and Andy Forrest who became my close friends.

I found my job with the railway challenging. I had to be there at 5 a.m. to get train reports and call crews for the 6 a.m. departure of the St. Paul-Winnipeg passenger train, known as the Soo Line Flyer. Then there was overtime involved with stock trains moving to markets in the United States, which required speedy transfer to the Soo Line and Great Northern Railway.

I still found time to play baseball and there were dances and other entertainment in the town and countryside as I met many new friends. Almost immediately, the British Empire Service League, forerunner of the Royal Canadian Legion, was formed. The Emerson district, known as branch No. 77, boasted a fine membership. Bolstered by veterans from the neighbouring towns of Dominion City, Letellier, Ridgeville and others, we had a strong voice in our municipalities. With over fifty members, we were dedicated to preserving the memory of our fallen comrades, the principles of comradeship and the sincere theme of peace, which is just as important today as it was then. (Never again must always be our motto.)

The British Empire Service League effectively ran the town. The League, on which I served two terms as president, was linked to the town council, school board and church groups. It was the strength of

the town. There was no question. We also lobbied successfully for veterans to receive priority in filling vacant government positions, especially in Customs and Immigration departments, in this border town. We also organized parties, baseball tournaments and social events.

Now, with my work and community activities established, my thoughts turned to finding a partner and establishing a home of my own. I had come home from the war expecting to share my life with Kathleen Ginn, who I grew up with in Dominion City. She was my girl before I headed overseas. However, I didn't see much of her when I came back. Her family moved down to Texas for a little while before re-acquiring their Dominion City-area farm. Kathleen and I had parted ways amicably and remained friends as she married another man but then, sadly, died giving birth for the first time.

I was anxious to meet someone new. I wanted someone who had the blessing of family members, was a gentle person, and shared my religious faith, love of outdoor activities, and understood love worked both ways in the area of work and play.

Mother had a friend in Emerson, Mrs. Emily Bell, who would quickly become known to me as "Auntie Bell." They had become close through church circles in Dominion City and Emerson. Emily and her husband Frank did not have any children of their own but they were generous and good people and they took in all young people that came in contact with them. Frank's duties as an immigration officer took him to the international trains that operated between border stations. Emily was often alone so, along with her great church and community activities, she also took boarders — usually young women school teachers. She was famous for her generosity, immaculate home and outstanding hospitality, patriotism, respect for veterans, cooking and dining etiquette. I knew of her quite well because she was awfully good to the veterans. She often had them in for dinner, but I didn't have any occasion to meet Auntie Bell before one very memorable evening. She invited me to have dinner and meet her niece.

Her niece was a pretty school teacher who had transferred to

Emerson from Winnipeg. I hastened to accept. As I recall, I gave up a baseball practice that night, but baseball's importance faded considerably after that life-changing dinner of destiny. I think I fell in love with Margaret Bell Hooper the night I met her. There were just the four of us, Frank and Emily Bell, Margaret Hooper and myself. I can't tell you what the delightful meal was. I know it must have been enjoyable, but all I ever saw was "Margie" as her auntie called her, with her beautiful long brown hair, soft grey eyes, and smooth pink complexion and soft voice.

After dinner, Margie, an accomplished pianist, played lively and romantic music and we sang along to the more popular songs. After a splendid evening, I wanted to learn a lot more about this attractive teacher. We said good night early. I didn't kiss her in person but I did in my imagination. That first impression grew, I can tell you honestly, and love took over. I asked her if I could see her again but what I didn't know was that she was dating a young farmer in Emerson. However, she agreed to see me again.

You could say our love story began with a love story. Our next "appointment" was to see a silent movie in town. It was a serial show over five or six evenings. After seeing one episode of Diamond in the Sky, we just had to see them all. We came to an understanding that, to see the show through, I had to be going steady with her. When you have a girlfriend, you stick with her and don't take somebody else to the show. I had decided then and there that she was the one for me. I hadn't proposed to her or anything like that but it looked to me like I was pretty well in love with her all right. How did I know? From the happiness I had in being in her company. I liked everything about her. She came from a good family and I thought she was acceptable to my family. She was a very pretty girl.

Margaret told me she had been seeing the farmer but was not anymore. "Confidentially," she said, "I am not interested in a farming life." It didn't take me long to know Marg was the one for me.

When the show finished, with a happy ending, we were pretty well

cemented. I saw her every chance I could get. We went to plays, dances and sporting events.

In the weeks that followed, I learned much about my girl. Margaret Hooper had come to Emerson from Winnipeg to stay at the home of her Aunt Emily and Uncle Frank. Frank was her mother's brother and she had often come to this home as a girl to visit the aunt and uncle she dearly loved. There is a photo post card that Auntie Bell had made and sent to Margaret in Winnipeg. It shows Margaret (about five) with her mother in Auntie's garden, and the note begins "Auntie's little girl." My daughters consider this card a treasure.

It was Auntie Bell and Uncle Frank who had persuaded the young Normal School graduate to apply for the primary grade

HAPPY COUPLE: Margaret and I enjoy a visit to my family's farm near Dominion City in 1921, the year we were married.

Spear Family Photo

position in the Emerson School District. Her job paid sixty dollars per month. She gave half of that to Auntie and Uncle. She was like their daughter and remained so all of their lives.

My Margaret was the eldest of three daughters, along with Dorothy and Jean, born to John and Margaret Anne Hooper. The Hoopers were a very well known family in Winnipeg. John's father Samuel designed and supervised the construction of several provincial buildings in Winnipeg. He created the University of Manitoba's first building, the

legislature, and city hall. Most of his work still stands today. He was also a sculptor and engraver and, at one time, owned the Hooper Marble Works in Winnipeg. It was Samuel who fashioned the monument of Queen Victoria, which stood in front of City Hall. John, Margaret's father, was also creative and developed several Winnipeg landmarks.

Moore's Restaurant was quite a contemporary design. Their marble stones and works can be seen in several memorial parks across Canada.

Margaret's mother had been a music teacher, like mine. Margaret, Dorothy, and Jean enjoyed a very special childhood with their grandparents lavishing attention on them. They told me about Sunday afternoon rides in their grandparents' fashionable carriage and, later, a motor car.

Margaret went to Kelvin High School. She then

MY SPECIAL GALS: I'm the centre of attention in this 1921 photo at Dominion City with Margaret, left, and my sister Helen, right.
Spear Family Photo

FARM FUN: Margaret, left, Helen, centre, and my dad get close during our visit to the family farm near Dominion City in 1921.
Spear Family Photo

attended the Manitoba Normal School, where she acquired her teaching credential. Her parents saw to it that she had instruction in the piano, for she was very talented, and she continued in that splendid interest all of her life.

There was no thought of sexual intercourse. The approach we took to our relationship was really high. Over the weeks and months, as we learned to know one another and talked of our hopes and dreams, I knew she was the one for me. We went steady for about six months before another fateful evening. I was invited to Auntie Bell's quite often. One night, we were smooching (I told Tom Snyder we were "sparking") on the couch with the oil lamp turned down low. Auntie Bell came in the living room and surprised us. She was pretty mad about the lamp. It was a lamp that didn't show much light. Why we turned it down I can never tell you. She was very upset with Margie for doing such a thing. I came to Margaret's rescue. "I want you to know, Auntie, that Marge and I are going to get married." She hugged us joyfully. "Now, you can blow out the light," she said. However, Marge didn't exactly say yes. "Perhaps you had better ask my father," she advised.

Well, I wasn't marrying her father. I was marrying her, but that was the protocol in those days. He came down to Emerson from Winnipeg and, when he was going home on the train, he said, "We'll see" and that was the end of that, I thought, but Marge said her dad thought he gave consent.

That's the way it worked in those days. I don't suppose it made a lot of difference. I would have married her anyway. On a bright September 17, 1921, our wedding took place in the Central Congregational Church in Winnipeg. The Reverend George Lawton and my father presided over the ceremony. It was marvelous. I couldn't have wished it any other way. I started a trend that would also see Dad marry off Wallace and Helen. I wore a navy blue suit with a white shirt. I didn't wear a hat — I had a good head of hair then — but almost everyone wore hats in those days. I had highly polished black button boots — the

rage in those days. The ladies used to have them and the men thought that was great too.

My bride looked elegant and lovely in a stylish, navy suit and a magnificent navy velvet hat trimmed with ostrich feathers. Her aunts Elizabeth and Emma, who were professional dressmakers, fashioned her wardrobe. Margaret's sister Dorothy and my brother Wallace stood up for us while both our families were happily approving. We said standard wedding vows, concluded by "Let no man put asunder . . ." The bond, which would continue for the rest of our lives, was tied.

We went right from the church to the train to depart for our honeymoon in Minneapolis. There weren't that many cars in those days but a lot of people came to the train station to see us off. We went through Emerson to Minneapolis. There was a big crowd at Emerson. We got off the train and stayed there for about thirty minutes as the train changed engines. They brought rice and party favours.

In Minneapolis, we stayed at the Drake Hotel. It cost what then might have been considered an outrageous five dollars a night, but we would have paid one hundred. We were madly in love and money was just a necessity to live.

Before our wedding, Marge and I made plans to live in a triplex, a two-storey unit near both the CPR station and Auntie and Uncle's place. We painted, scrubbed, papered and modified the central area to fit our needs. We furnished it with the best that money could buy: quite modern, professionally chosen furnishings, cabinets, window coverings — and a Mason and Riche piano. I had one thousand dollars in the bank after we had furnished our first home. The rent was ten dollars per month.

Enjoying my work, our town, a comfortable home, and living with a beautiful young woman who showed much care and affection, I was sitting on top of the world. We both knew we were very fortunate indeed.

We became part of a lively community very quickly. Hockey and curling in the winter and baseball in the summer had always been

important to me and I continued to compete. Marge came right along with me. The wives and families of other players came too. We were all part of the hometown gang.

I thought my future was made. Marge was in her third year of her contract with the Emerson School District when we were married. She had to surrender her position because no women were allowed to hold jobs if their husbands were employed. We were both aware of that provision and knew that it would be necessary for me to work harder. How would women feel about such a rule today?

Marge kept herself busy by maintaining her interest in music. She played the piano in a dance orchestra and, for a while, in a silent movie theatre. Later she would become the long-time organist for St. Andrews United Church.

We spoke about our plans for our children long before they came. (One of the first things I did was take out a $50,000 life insurance policy, to ensure that they would be looked after if anything happened to me.) We wanted them to have the best education possible — university training. It was a real plan of life. We wanted to ensure they had quality living and quality purposes.

Marge and I also emphasized this approach with our future generations. Some of my grandchildren have obtained university degrees. I'm sure my great-grandchildren will also excel in their educational pursuits, too. Today, many parents buy mini-vans for their young families but we had fewer options as we started thinking about buying a motor car in 1922, when we discovered we were going to have a family. The local garage proprietor, a great baseball booster by the name of Shay Buckman, thought he had the right car for me. It was a 1913 Olds Hupmobile, a touring car with side-curtains on the windows. It was a real quality car with a self-starter on the dash. A pump for inflating tires was connected to the motor, and a spare tire rested on the rear end bracket. They were low pressure tires but they still had their own inner tubes. You always carried a spare tire in the back and a cloth-like material to put patches on tires, a pump and a jack. The jack was always

very necessary. Balloon tires came in around 1923 or 1924.

Most cars had a crank on the front of it, but you had to set the spark. In the car, there was a spark lever and the gas feed was with your hand on the wheel. There was no gas pedal. We inserted the gasoline in the rear of the tank and we measured the fuel level with a dip stick. We had a spare one-gallon tank that we mounted right on the front.

All this for eight hundred and fifty dollars. We bought it, loved it and enjoyed the rare convenience of a garage in the rear of our terrace. We learned how to service and care for our deluxe transportation, but what a pain it was to get the car jacked up — even though we had a super-sized jack for the emergency. We would have several flat tires during our five years of ownership but it was our first car and very special. Gas was about twenty-five cents a gallon and cars could get twenty to twenty-five miles per gallon so the expense for this pleasure was minimal. We seldom missed a day in summer when we didn't go someplace for picnics, ball games or family visits.

(In the winter, because we didn't have anti-freeze, we put our car up on blocks, took the battery out and put it in the basement. We also received a rebate on our license fee for six months.)

There were no medical or driving tests necessary to obtain a license in those days. The roads in and around Emerson were usually closed for the winter because of snow. There was no road maintenance crew to keep them clear, except for one on Highway 75 between Winnipeg and Minneapolis. Even this highway was a dirt road until the 1930s, when one side was gravelled and sided by one-inch planking. We really thought these upgrades were great improvements, but driving was still dicey when the gravel disappeared into poor grading. However, Highway 75 was open all summer and would allow us to visit the Hoopers in Winnipeg often.

PREPARING FOR CHANGE

We were thrilled with the knowledge that we would soon be parents and we took trips to Winnipeg and Dominion City — all on dirt

roads. When Marge's due date approached, we decided she would go to the Winnipeg General Hospital for the birth so that Mother and Dad Hooper would be close by. The due date was going to be well into December when weather would be uncertain. We went to Winnipeg about ten days before the calculated date and I returned to Emerson. Our decision proved to be a good one because, when the call came, it was one of the coldest nights I can ever remember — at least thirty below Fahrenheit. I took the way freight train in time to be with Marge and, just before midnight on December 17, 1922, our first little daughter, Margaret Joyce Spear, was born. (She goes by Joyce.) Mother and daughter were fine and beautiful so I could happily leave them to be home in Emerson for my shift starting at five o'clock the next morning.

I remember going to the home of Jim Percival, a conductor on the southbound Soo Line. We walked in vicious weather to the CPR yard office where trains were marshalled and we left quickly, hoping to make the deadline. The engine crew and dispatchers were aware I was on that train and they helped me along the way, making sure I was on time. Back at the station, everyone expressed good wishes as the news of our newborn spread. Calls to Auntie Bell and Dominion City in the early hours brought great happiness and relief. I returned to our home after work and slept very well.

Ten days later, Marge and Joyce came home. It was so comforting to have them close and well. Throughout that winter, we were very protective and stayed in our cozy, warm quarters. We played bridge with our good friends the Coulters and a new game call mah jong. I still played hockey. (I'll tell you more about my sporting pursuits in a later chapter.)

In 1924, we had a chance to purchase a home closer to the centre of town, a bit farther from work but only a block away from Auntie and Uncle. Mr. Jake Empey, a retired farmer and carpenter of some skill, had rebuilt a two-bedroom bungalow and we liked everything about it. There was a large garden, a garage, and an outbuilding which had been

NEW WHEELS: My daughter Joyce and I take a rest on the stoop of my new 1926 Chevrolet in front of our home in Emerson, Manitoba.   Spear Family Photo

a small sturdy barn with roller doors — all on an excellent corner lot.

A splendid town well was one block away — a big plus, because we depended on wells for our drinking and cooking water, which had to be fetched daily. We settled on a price of three thousand dollars with a down payment of fifteen hundred dollars and twenty-five dollars per month for the next two years. The taxes were about twenty-five dollars per year, about average for residents in that area.

Marge was a wonderful homemaker, inside and outside, and her ideas really stood out in the improvements that we initiated. We planted hedges; made minor repairs to the garage; and painted, cleaned and wired the outbuilding. A couple of years later we would add a glassed-in porch along the front of the house and install striped awnings wonderful window boxes along the side to make it very attractive home. We became very proud of our home.

(I still have a picture of it but, unfortunately, the house was swept away in the Red River flood in the 1950s — after we left Emerson.)

In 1925, I was recruited by the Canadian Cadet Corps to organize a company in Emerson. I received a small remuneration, and all the

equipment necessary to erect a range for .22-calibre rifles, modelled after the short Lee Enfield service rifle, which I was familiar with from my army days. A captain from Winnipeg headquarters came down and we discussed recruitment. Cadets had to be fifteen to nineteen years old under the program endorsed by the federal government.

We rented a long, rambling vacant building known as the Immigration Hall. It was only a long block from the CPR station, and the top floor had an area suitable for a thirty-five yard shooting range. Proper steel backboards were shipped from Winnipeg and the ten-alley range was completed with all approvals in place. I recruited about ten or twelve boys who were interested in wearing uniforms and doing some army training. They used the beautiful rifles to test their shooting skills in competitions with other cadet units across Manitoba, including Winnipeg.

Within a year, we had thirty boys meeting every Monday night at the shooting range, which also served as the winter drill grounds where I conducted exercises according to army regulations. The boys liked the promise of summer camp in tents. The strict orders that were enforced on the range also held for the parade grounds. Uniforms were issued and the boys showed considerable interest when exams (mostly oral) came around for promotion. Some people objected to the military con-notation but, to me, it was a good experience for the young men to learn how to handle firearms responsibly and skillfully. Every effort was made to ensure safety and there were no accidents.

Now, ten years before the Second World War, it also looked like another war was in the making and patriotic organizations and town officials were behind the cadet program. The opposition subsided as the cadets displayed their professionalism and showed very well in the rifle competitions. We were fourth in the British Empire on one or two occa-sions and one of our members won a trip to Bisley, England.

We also became very involved with St. Andrews United Church. Marge sang in the choir and played the organ. I would serve as secre-tary-treasurer of the board for many years. We were both very friendly

with the young ministers and their wives who came to serve there. Our church involvement would continue for our twenty years in Emerson.

In 1926, I was promoted to train dispatcher in Winnipeg and was called on for relief work, mostly in the fall season, and that took our family to Marge's home at 484 McDermott Avenue. This was a very happy change. Mrs. Hooper was a sweet woman who made us very welcome. Daughter and mother had a wonderful visit. Marge's parents and sisters made a great fuss over Joyce and the meals were marvelous. Jean was still living at home and Dody was there sometimes too, which made for some spirited talk.

The Hoopers had a crystal radio set and over the airwaves and through the headset came delightful music and conversation. On one occasion, Jean placed the headset on Joyce. "He's talking to me," she excitedly proclaimed. "Is he talking to you?" I think, perhaps, it was Santa Claus.

I had an opportunity to stay in Winnipeg but the position wasn't guaranteed. Pleasant as those times were, I opted for a permanent stay in Emerson because I could see that Joyce would soon have to attend school regularly. So back to our permanent residence in Emerson we went.

Margaret and I learned we were going to be parents again. Everything had to be ready. To begin with, we purchased a Maytag electric washing machine with automatic wringers. Hot water had to come from the stove reservoir, but it was still simply wonderful. We did not yet have running water. A pump was our tap. A coal-burning furnace and a wood-burning stove supplied our heat. Our refrigerator was actually an ice box and a dumb waiter that descended into the cool depths of the basement via a pulley system. Most of the other homes had such contrivances, which really were quite workable. (Eventually, we had running water, a second cistern and an electric refrigerator and stove. At this stage, we felt fairly advanced.)

Marge decided she would like to have a home birth with a nurse and the doctor attending. This time, winter had passed and April was the

JOINING GENERATIONS: My mother Margaret Ballingal Spear, standing next to my father, has her hands full with granddaughters Dorothy (in her arms) and Joyce.
Spear Family Photo

due time. We contacted Nurse Sarah Brown and prepared the setting. When Marge felt the time was near, I took our new 1926 Chevrolet down River Road to pick up Sarah. The good lady was already packed, smiling and full of optimism. I wanted to help, but I was of precious little assistance because I was a nervous wreck holding on for dear life. Dr. McIntosh came by and suggested I take Joyce over to Auntie Bell's, which had been pre-arranged. It was dark as I carried my little sleeping daughter over to the care of her dear aunt. It was a very long night. At one o'clock in the afternoon of April 13, 1928, our second little daughter appeared. Dorothy Helen Spear (now Pike) was a perfect, happy baby. The first to know was Auntie, who now had a second child to love and caress for her nearly very own. Auntie really loved Marge as her own daughter and our children became her "grandchildren."

89

HOOD ORNAMENTS: My daughters Joyce, left, and Dorothy, right, pose on the front of our car in front of our home in Emerson, Manitoba in the 1920s.

We strove to provide a good, solid Christian home life and many activities in the church and community, in which they were very involved and real leaders. Right from the time that they started going to school, we insisted that they should go to university and get a higher education — and strive for that. Not too many people in Emerson went to university in those days. Joyce and Dorothy had to develop a real desire to get there. We kept them busy studying and sought good companionship, good leadership and exceptionally good reading materials for them.

Joyce particularly took to good literary work. Dorothy was an exceptionally good student too. They graduated with honours. Joyce got a fellowship at the University of Minnesota and later taught at the University of Pittsburgh before moving to California with her first husband Edward Worthington. Dorothy would marry Ron Pike and their

path would lead to Calgary, our current hometown.

My advice to you? Take part in all of your children's activities, teach them moral laws and give them great support and love. They will develop a desire to excel. Remember: If it's going to be, it's up to me.

I took my children right into my life. Even in later years, we played a lot of golf together, skated together and curled together. Growing up, Joyce and Dorothy knew where I was all the time. They knew what I was doing because I was on the road a lot. I worked very early hours and then spent afternoons with them. You have to plan your goals for your children right from day one. Indicate right from the start that they're going to university. Give them good guidance. Live a good life yourself and promote theirs. Encourage them in everything they do and include them in as many of your activities as possible. Keep a complete interest in something until such time as they've developed a love for it themselves. We always took the girls on our holidays, which were quite extensive because I had access to transportation on the railways.

The demands of parenthood sometimes got pretty lofty but they paid off too. We took them to places where it cost us a little money and we provided good places to live. They developed a taste for the better than average things in life.

I tried to set an example by excelling in my work. It's a wonderful thing to have your children proud of you. We developed a pretty fine life, I tell you. It worked out very well. We emphasized the highest quality of life in every aspect — honesty, integrity, desire, fulfillment, pride! Set your standards pretty high.

We had a love for the better things in life and were able to maintain a good quality of life. We had complete understanding and forgiveness. We were willing to listen, learn and, as you'll discover in a later chapter, we were able to close ranks around tragedy. There was no drinking or carousing. As a family, we disagreed but we didn't quarrel. Most disagreements come from a shortage of funds, things that you can't afford. We worked to afford them. If there's something you really want to acquire to improve your children's lives, cut the family budget to get

it.

Our lives were very simple. We gave up a lot for the girls and enjoyed doing it. It was a pleasure to see them excel. Their success made for better living. We gave up holidays or something that we wanted ourselves. I took every opportunity to progress in my career in order to give Joyce and Dorothy a good education. They knew that too. I got a great deal of enjoyment from sacrifice and doing things properly and well — and still do. This enjoyment comes from just knowing that I'm helping somebody, that I'm making some- body's life happier. We enjoy very close family relations on all sides of the family.

Do we even get along with in- laws? Well, there was never any doubt about that. There was just a complete melding. Even today, there are very strong ties. Love is

HAMMING IT UP: My kid brother Wallace, right, now over one hundred years old, and I enjoy some laughs with my daughter Joyce in the 1930s at Dominion City. Spear Family Photo

the governing factor in all our gatherings. It's just a deep respect for family, which continues to inspire me today.

I've just got a calm feeling about living at my age. Life is very smooth-flowing. I'm in a position to understand other people's diffi- culties. I live in total comfort. I feel very secure. I'm willing to under- stand other people. I'll make a lot of allowances for people who didn't have the upbringing that I had. Of course, I've had a lot of help along the way from my parents, Marge's parents, Auntie Bell and other

friends and relatives too numerous to mention, but one lady really stood out. My grandmother.

Agnes Laird Ballingal, my mother's mother, always wore a pretty lace cap, a Scottish lady's custom. She had emigrated from Scotland to Paris, Ontario, with her aunt and uncle in 1844, when she was ten years old. Her husband died relatively young and she came from Galt, Ontario, to live with us when she was sixty-four years old. She stayed in our home for about nineteen years while I was there. My brothers and sister and I just grew up with her. She lived with my parents for forty years. We were amazed by anything she did. We were very proud of her.

She was a second mother and she commanded — and earned — great respect. She was a tremendous influence in our home. Everyone loved her and respected her because of one obvious attribute: Her attitude. She was an extremely happy person, always very comforting, and always optimistic. She was always so active. She was interested in everything. It wasn't home without Grannie. I have inherited many of my traits from her. (When I was overseas during World War I, she wrote many loving and comforting letters to me and helped me get through it.)

Anything that I have today at my age is infinitesimal in comparison to Grannie's accomplishments around the turn of the twentieth century. Even in her late eighties, she never complained and always took care of us when Mother and Dad were away performing their church duties at choir practice, prayer meetings, Ladies Aid services, Temperance Society meetings, Odd Fellows Lodge, weddings, baptisms and funerals.

Grannie became the "chief" of our home. She was such a great lady, loved and respected by all for her ways with the sewing needle and in the kitchen. Because she was there, Mother and Dad enjoyed worry-free relationships with their congregation. I can't remember a single instance where Grannie gave a poor report of our conduct when our parents returned. My mother and her mother were always very close

and loved being together. She loved my father like a son and he held her in the highest esteem. There were never any mother-in-law jokes in our home.

Everyone loved to be near Grannie. She didn't have the ability to maintain herself in her later years but Mother and Dad gave her all she would ever need. I can never remember her ever having a doctor. There were no nursing homes in those days but, even if there were, I doubt she would have gone to one. What better could she have than her daughter or son-in-law? They were so good to her.

Grannie must have had a very happy soul because she never complained about anything. She just seemed to be happy in her security, never tolerating liquor or smoking. Grannie was just a gentle lady awaiting God's call, dispensing love and so willing to talk of modern things. She kept up with the times by reading. She was very proud of being able to converse and to be with friends. She loved company. Her mind was clear. It was a very remarkable occurrence that she wasn't ill — she was just old.

Grannie was extremely proud of herself. She didn't demand any attention — but she received more than many people could expect at that time in Canada's history, when communication and transportation systems were much less sophisticated than they are today.

She became a very highly respected lady in Manitoba, especially around election time. She was always a Liberal. Every year after her hundredth year, she was always recognized by the government of Canada. When I received certificates for my hundredth birthday, from Prime Minister Jean Chretien and Queen Elizabeth, I thought of the honours bestowed upon her. When I make appearances on television or at public speaking engagements, I'm often reminded of the notoriety she received in her day, an era when electricity was considered a luxury. Her crowning achievement came in 1929, as she celebrated her one hundred and second birthday in Dominion City. The Scottish Society of Manitoba rented an airplane and invited her to go up for a sightseeing tour to celebrate her birthday and Scottish heritage. Grannie accepted

right away. She was always extremely interested in progress, so we weren't surprised that she would go. She was just delighted to think that she was going to have a flight.

I don't think the event was very well advertised but everybody in town showed up. There were about one hundred people watching. I was there with my family. My daughter, Joyce, now in her seventies, was about five. Dorothy, also in her seventies, was a year old. It was a biplane and reminded me of the airplanes we flew in

HIGH FLYERS: Grannie's flight with Dad in a byplane on her 102nd birthday made her a media darling. She didn't like this photo though. Spear Family Photo

the war except it wasn't a fighter. You had to, as the old saying goes, make contact as you cranked the propeller. It was a pretty dangerous deal. Only one person, the pilot, could swing the prop. It didn't take more than one pull. The engine coughed a little but started right up. As far as I know it was the first time a plane ever flew out of there with passengers.

Alvin Keith took them up. He was a barnstorming pilot. I believe he

flew in World War I. We always said he did anyway. Everybody stood in the middle of a field at the town's exhibition grounds and looked to the sky as Grannie and Dad's plane buzzed along at about five thousand feet and circled the country outside of the town for thirty to forty minutes. It was Grannie's first — and last — flight ever and it made town history. The fact that she was that age and would take to the air in an open aircraft generated enormous attention. The picture of Dad and Grannie, taken that day, which you also see in here, was in every newspaper around. The Winnipeg Free Press was there to record the occasion.

In her later years, she wasn't able to get around that well. She was usually in a wheelchair but, getting around with a cane that day, why, that was pretty damn good. The only comment that I remember from Grannie was: "I don't like that picture, David. It makes me look too old. You were holding me up."

Two years later, in 1931, Grannie died at home in her sleep. No fewer than five hundred people, from the surrounding countryside and as far away as Winnipeg, came to pay their respects. I was a regional freelance reporter with the Winnipeg Free Press at the time, reporting on community and sports events, and I wrote her obituary. She lies next to Dad and Mother in Dominion City. Her tombstone reads: "She died as she lived, believing in God."

THE GREAT DEPRESSION

Around the time of Grannie's death, in the 1930s, my family and I started to experience many changes. We saw the dawn of nearly ten years of depression for Canada and the war clouds on the horizon were getting darker and darker. It was a terrible depression. We didn't know how long it was going to last. Canadian railway traffic dropped dramatically, particularly the interchange between Canadian and American railroads. Layoffs and closures of stations created fear of job losses and government railway-related positions were in jeopardy. One day in 1935, there was an exchange of just one car on the Soo Line whereas

twenty- five to thirty usually ran along it. Movement on other subdivisions and regional lines decreased dramatically. The CPR gave all their respective unions — firemen, conductors, station agents and operators — an ultimatum. All employees could take a ten per cent pay cut or the company would close stations, abolish positions and reduce train schedules to fit the traffic. A strike at this point was seen as a poor way to settle the problem and employees wisely accepted the reduced pay and stayed employed. I was grateful just to be able to go to work. Not everybody has he opportunity to go to work and get paid for something they love to do.

Still the lower pay, effective immediately, gave us all a scare and showed just how vulnerable we all were to the Depression that was upon us. The evidence was everywhere. There was quite an exodus to the United States. Ford Motor Company took about ten people from our town. They went to work in the automobile plant in Detroit for five dollars per day. Those boys never came back to Canada.

More and more young men were hitching rides on the rail cars and getting off along the way to seek farm jobs for a day or a week. Meanwhile, there was an increasing number of men going through the towns and asking for food. We always provided for the young and not so young. We were a young family with children growing up and going to school in a town of about five hundred people. We tightened our budgets, forgot about new cars, stayed home during holidays, and depended on our gardens for more vegetables. We even grew celery. (It had to be covered so it wouldn't burn in the sun.) We also grew corn and lots of potatoes. Margaret was a great homemaker. She was an expert in home economics so she was pretty well equipped for reducing costs in the home. We learned how to store food for winter and we made and canned our jams, jellies and relishes.

DAUGHTERS' EDUCATION

Our desire and determination to succeed made it all possible. There was never any doubt in our minds that the children came first. We never

lost faith in our plans for Joyce and Dorothy. They held us together. The girls had common training in school, church circles and Sunday school and they both held prominent positions as they grew up. They certainly made my life desirable and we worked very closely together financially, spiritually, religiously and socially.They made great friends with their teachers. We were welcome in their teachers' homes and they gave us great assistance.

The merchants felt a severe pinch, although we tried to give them as much business as we could. Emerson was, in fact, quite fortunate to have so many government and railway-related paycheques still being paid.

Other towns did not fare as well as we did. Crops were poor. Farmers were getting almost nothing, approximately thirty cents a bushel for wheat. So much of our economy relied on farm products, particularly grains. Of those, wheat was the precious commodity. When the price of wheat fell considerably, the effect was devastating. The farmers, for the most part, had to hope and pray for rain and warm weather at the right time. Even if the crops were plentiful, the take was much lower. My parents relied heavily now on the sale of grain for their livelihood. My father continued to act as pastor but was paid mostly in goods — chickens, eggs, meats, baking — and services. It was a wonderful blessing to have the farm as a backup. We learned to do things for ourselves and took great pride in doing that. Despite the difficult times, we took great joy in everything we did. We upheld each other. I learned to be self-sufficient — very much so.

Even during the Depression, my life was always progressive. I made sure I had lots of things to do. We maintained our church obligations and our community obligations. I was chairman of the United Church's board of stewards for many years. I was also elected as a school board trustee for two terms and, about 1934, I was nominated for a position on the town council. I was still on the school board but withdrew to compete for the council and was fortunate to win the election in our ward. The town required an assessor and I was nominated for that posi-

tion. I had one year to revise the assessment of all residential and business properties according to the revised code.

It was a very unpopular job, as one can imagine. I studied the code and interviewed all owners and property tax payers and came up with quite an acceptable plan, which was accepted by council with little revision. It was fair and it became the new law set for cities and towns in Manitoba — and it worked. I wrote the Big Book in my own handwriting. I was paid one hundred dollars for that year's work.

Back on the town council, I was next appointed chairman of the light and power commission. Here I was really into something big. We had been dickering with the Manitoba Power Commission for a line of power from Winnipeg and were successful in getting a contract for about five cents a kilowatt hour. We sold this for around ten cents per kilowatt hour to subscribers. We had conversations with our American friends and councillors in Pembina, North Dakota and St. Vincent, Minnesota, towns located about three miles south of Emerson and secured an excellent contract with them. For a few years, we made over ten thousand dollars annually for our town.

Eventually, an American power company ran lines from power stations in Grand Forks, North Dakota, and our supply was no longer needed but, for a time, Emerson reaped the benefits of this profitable export.

Thanks to securing electrical services, stove, light, refrigerator and even car heater sales boomed. We were an up and coming town of conveniences. I made extra money by sending sports, weather and community reports to the Winnipeg Free Press and the Winnipeg Tribune. I gathered the data with simple weather instruments — a rain gauge, thermometer and meteorological box. Some of those snow levels and temperature readings were records. Temperatures reached forty below (celsius or fahrenheit, since they both measure the same at that point) while snow drifts occasionally blocked the front and back doors of our homes. On those early morns of blizzard conditions, I was glad to have my dog Mac accompany me on the walk to work at half past four. Some

of those trips could chill my bones, despite a warm overcoat, gauntlets, scarves and a cap that came down over my ears and brow.

Marge was always worried about my getting to the station, as long mile away. I appreciated her concern and called her on reaching my destination. I never did miss getting there on time. It was so important to rouse the crew and stoke the furnace in the station before the men came on duty and boarded the train. Also, there were important messages to receive on the telegraph before the train came in.

I did two or three guys' work when they were laid off. It was mandatory. You had to do it or management would get someone else. I also worked as an assessor for a finance company to determine whether people could qualify for loans. Because I knew everybody so well, I would quietly advise the company on a loan applicant's home situation and assess their integrity and their ability to repay the loan. I probably examined about one hundred people. I received a small fee. Sometimes it didn't pay for my gasoline. I don't think I ever recommended turning anyone down.

Through these extra efforts, we always managed to save ten to twenty dollars per month and we put it away. At the end of ten years, we recognized our reward. Margaret had ten thousand dollars and I had ten thousand dollars and many years later we were later able to pay for a home in Calgary without the need for a mortgage.

Getting through the Depression gave me strong feelings of loyalty, security and determination. I felt loyalty to my home, to my church, to CPR workers and the company. The economic hardship was on your mind at all times. There were times when you thought it would never be over. The fact that I had job and financial security really boosted my ego. How fortunate we were compared to a lot of others. I learned the importance of always having something in reserve.

I've had an emergency plan all through my life. As a result of our Depression experiences, Margaret and I always had a very positive attitude and were able to overcome adversity very quickly and easily by showing sympathy and love and sharing our successes. The Depression

gave me a deep appreciation for life — a good life — and helped me prepare for more changes that were to come.

In 1938, Joyce completed her last year at Emerson Collegiate. She was slated to go to the University of Manitoba after Grade 11. (At that time, Grade 12 was equivalent to the first year of university.) We had consulted with our good friend, Mr. Bruce Moorehead, the principal of the high school, and he suggested that Joyce enroll in the department of home economics. She would later become a teacher. We made plans to have her enter the Department of Home Economics.

For the past ten years, all through the Great Depression, Marge had given six dollars and fifty cents every month out of her housekeeping money to Investors Syndicate. By 1938, the investment had generated one thousand dollars. This was to be used for tuition, books, and board at the university dormitory. In September, Marge and Dorothy and I went to Winnipeg to register Joyce and meet her instructors. That was a very proud occasion. We were so pleased to have our firstborn on her way in higher education. We were already planning that step for Dorothy too and she made us proud by obtaining a splendid education from Brandon College too.

We were very fortunate that both our daughters were interested in their studies and performed well in school. Beyond that, they were very loving and helpful young women, full of vitality and plans. They loved their home, their friends and their activities. They were active in Canadian Girls in Training; they skated, played tennis and golf. They both had excellent health and were relatively free from serious childhood diseases with the exception of chicken pox and measles.

As they grew into their teens, they were reasonable about our hopes and dreams for them. They knew we were holding out for lives of promise for them and, thus, we did not want them making any commitments for which they were not ready. We worried about this, as there were several young women in their age groups making their choices of mates, and this we wanted to avoid. It was hard, sometimes, to explain why we were so protective and why we hoped higher edu-

cational experiences would ensure a better chance for a more complete life. We felt it was important that Dorothy and Joyce know what was expected of them in terms of behaviour because they would soon be on their own. We hoped our ways would become automatic to them — but we didn't always see eye to eye.

One time, we forbade Joyce from going to a party at a home that we did not think was well supervised. "Why do you think we are better than anyone else?" she asked angrily. Our answer? We thought we were more careful. We told her we could not make a mistake with our children. We told her we were sorry if she was unhappy with our decision. She didn't go.

At any rate, both Joyce and Dorothy made us very proud parents as they excelled in all their endeavours. They were very good students and we budgeted for their schooling, post-secondary training and made their desire a success. We were always available for them and gave them financial aid. They did their part by seeking temporary employment to help themselves. They didn't disappoint us in any way. By being active in church and community life, we hoped our daughters would mirror our achievements in their own lives. We were careful with our funds but agreed on special needs that were important. We were as generous as we could be and I know both of them were very grateful for our loving kindness. They were extremely co-operative and they shared their successes with us. They made very strong friendships in school which have carried them right through their lives.

Our whole town responded well to the needs of our children and young adults in education, recreation and other healthful, stimulating pursuits. All of our incomes were greatly reduced, but we had homes, good food and gifted people who rose to the occasion and provided a good life in many areas. Our churches — United, Anglican, Baptist, Lutheran and Catholic — all rallied to make those places of worship a place to gather for socializing and good fellowship. All the great holy days became very important and all our congregations and leaders strived to make their music and their messages inspirational.

I will never forget the marvelous church potluck dinners when everyone brought something — and a lot of it. We still talk about Mrs. Cook's beet salad, Mrs. Templeton's chocolate cake, Marge's lemon meringue pie and Miss Tandy's pickles.

Margaret and I both had great faith in each other. We discovered that the simple things in life are the best. We had a very happy marriage. Marg was a very talented, beautiful woman who was advanced in her thinking. Although we disagreed at times, we had the family at heart. We were both very closely cemented with our home. We had great family gatherings and quality of life was quite high. We were married for life. We decided on that. We had our quarrels but we would forgive, forget, and love again. None of our disagreements involved infidelity. We never had any difficulty romancing each other. She was a wonderful lover. We were in love and we had so much to share with each other. There was never any danger of an open marriage (i.e. sharing partners.) I suppose we both had temptations to have sex with others but such desires were only fictitious.

Our formula proved itself to be very successful. We were both proud of our family heritage and we lived together with high principles and a good moral vision. We tried to be supportive of each other in every way. We trusted each other. Our love was a declaration of faithfulness. You have to give and take, so none of our disagreements threatened our marriage. There was never any talk of divorce. We didn't get that far. Divorce in those days was very unusual. I can never remember going to bed angry with each other. (You can't rest on a broken heart.) We had a deep respect for each other. It was just a question of where my authority ended and hers started. We just tried to make it mutual.

Our differences stemmed mostly from priority of time. During the first twenty years of our marriage, I rarely spent a night away from home without Margaret. My job didn't take me away from home and we always took the children on vacations together. Just the fact of leaving her alone bothered her. She understood that I was bonded to the Canadian Pacific. I guess she knew me better than I knew myself. She

knew that whenever I set out to do a job I would devote the time and effort that was necessary to succeed. The air force, during World War II, was a real test. My decision to enlist and serve my country a second time could easily have threatened our marriage — if we let it. Margaret understood that my desire to serve again was genuinely patriotic, a

AIR FORCE DAYS: Margaret and I stand in front of our Winnipeg home. My decision to join the air force upset her but she still supported me.

Spear Family Photo

compulsion to answer the call of duty, but she wasn't necessarily happy about my choice. There was danger involved to start with and I was leaving our family in Winnipeg. There was no promise that I wouldn't be sent overseas — thankfully, I stayed in Canada — because I signed up. When you sign up, you register for duty anywhere. I ranked the air force ahead of home and the girls. I was offered, and accepted, a commissioned rank in the Royal Canadian Air Force, based on my three and a half years of World War I service and my experience as commander of a cadet corps in Emerson, which had gained recognition in competitions within Manitoba.

After considerable prayer and soul searching, Margaret and I decided that we were in the war together. I parted ways with civilian life from March of 1941 until August of 1946. Our unified decision would prove to be a testament to enduring love, honour and patriotism and a stepping stone to future civilian opportunities. Margaret knew that I felt

I had a duty to do — and I did it. My duties were quite comparable to my civilian capabilities. Fortunately, I was able to enter service life quite smoothly and efficiently.

Margaret came with me as I was posted at various stations across Canada and advanced in rank from pilot officer to wing commander, the equivalent of acting lieutenant colonel. She showed support and understanding in all of our assignments and responsibilities, but she yearned for the

WING COMMANDER: I was proud to wear my air force uniform but, at the end of World War II, I decided family had to come first.   Spear Family Photo

day when we could return to our civilian lives and peacetime activities. She didn't like the military life. (I don't think the military and civilians co-operate very well. They live completely different lives. I know, as a ranking officer as well as a private, how happy the private soldier was when he got out of the service. He went right back to the ground floor and started all over again. The officer coming out of the army was a little different. He had been used to authority and I think it showed.)

In spirit, she was right with me all the way through. She did a splendid job. She made my life very happy in the air force. I met all the

demands anyway, and showed a lot of loyalty to my home. I was respected for my ways too. I was fortunate to have some pretty good officer friends. They fitted in with my ideals.

Our home life was shared with service personnel. That was very necessary. That was part of service life.

I was based at Winnipeg for three years and Souris, Manitoba, for two years. When I was appointed acting wing commander at Uplands, Ontario, which is now part of Ottawa, Margaret elected to return to our home in Winnipeg. I think she felt that was a critical time with Dorothy, while Joyce had moved to the United States.

I remained in Uplands for six months. That was the longest time that Margaret and I lived apart from one another but I could still get home to Winnipeg periodically.

My duties at Uplands included supplying aircraft to all commands of the Commonwealth Air Training Plan, from coast to coast. In May of 1945, we were on a flight to Western Air Command in Vancouver when we received an order to return to base. The war was over. When we arrived at Uplands, everyone was ecstatic. Everybody — or should I say almost everybody — couldn't wait to go home. Some wanted to have a career in the air force but most of the enlisted personnel were anxious to get back to their homes in all parts of Canada.

I received an exceptionally enticing offer to remain in the permanent air force as a senior officer until I qualified for a pension — possibly within six or seven years. The chance to stay in the air force was certainly something to consider, but not for long after Marge got wind of it. She was not going to have any part in the air force. She opted instead for my immediate and honourary discharge.

Meanwhile, the Canadian Pacific Railway had issued a recall to duty. If I didn't return within a month, I would lose my seniority. I was glad to get back into civvies. The air force vice-marshal and Air Command dispatched two wonderful letters of appreciation for my five and a half years of exemplary service to the president of the CPR. (I was recommended for the Order of the British Empire, for service to the com-

monwealth, three times and my last nomination was being considered when the war ended.) I believe these were instrumental in my future promotions within the company.

However, they also probably set the stage for the next biggest challenge to my marriage. My transition back to civilian life was more difficult than I had assumed it would be. It became a real challenge. My CPR seniority had to be re-established and confirmed by the Order of Railway Telegraphers. After that, I would face what was known as the rule of qualification — without pay — for the train dispatcher's position to which I was entitled on the Portage, Brandon or Kenora divisions. The train dispatcher had more responsibility. The rules and working conditions had changed. The train engines were more powerful and I had to acquaint myself with train dispatching operations at the highest level. The requirement to re-qualify was reasonable — the dispatcher position was a very important job — but I felt I should have been paid for it.

My seniority meant a great deal to me because that was your ticket to a promotion. When the job became vacant, the senior man got it.

I had a real love for railroading and had a desire for excellence. I settled in at first on the Portage Division and, after two weeks of supervision at all positions in that dispatching office, I was assigned to a temporary position in the Brandon Division Dispatching Office as I awaited a permanent placement that my seniority commanded.

My Brandon posting turned out to be an extremely happy return to dispatching duties. About six months later, my seniority, which included the years I was away in the air force, was restored. Giving employees an opportunity to keep their seniority after war service (as long as they were healthy and re-qualified for their positions) was a patriotic gesture on the part of the Canadian Pacific.

We developed some excellent, lifelong friendships as we met new co-workers and moved from our lovely home in Winnipeg, but the shift was very disruptive to the schooling of our daughters and our home life. Dorothy came with us and enrolled at Brandon College while

HOME ON RAILS: This fully equipped instruction car took me across Western Canada during my tenure as rules examiner for the CPR's Prairie and Pacific region.

Joyce was away at the University of Minnesota. As usual, Margaret took over the family responsibility, providing loving care and supervision at home while I awaited a permanent dispatcher position.

Our social life was still really happy and constructive and we made friendships that would last all our lives. We had rented out our home in Winnipeg on a temporary contract and, within a year, a retirement in the Winnipeg office allowed me to claim a day trick — 9 a.m. to 5 p.m. My advanced seniority, which included my war service, was the key factor in obtaining this position. We happily returned to Winnipeg with great expectations. I had the first day job in my life.

I had a strong desire to advance and I was interviewed by the CPR's general manager, J. I. McKay. He was supportive of my aspirations and, within a few months, a reorganization of railway rules — designed to improve safety — opened the door to a rules examiner's position.

In 1951, I was appointed rules examiner for the Portage Division, which had nine branch lines, including Winnipeg. Later that year, I was

promoted to rules instructor for the Manitoba district. On April 1, 1954, I was named rules instruct for the prairie and Pacific districts, extending from Winnipeg to Vancouver Island. I was provided with an instruction car, which was equipped with a small classroom. I travelled across the divisions as I instructed, examined and certified employees, ensuring that they knew the operating rules. From time to time, I rode at the head end of the train with the employees. Each employee had to be re-examined every three years. I was allowed to set my own schedules and reported to the western region superintendent from time to time.

During these years, Joyce came home to marry Edward Worthington, a chemical engineer who was one of the most intelligent men I ever met. Again my father was one of the officiating clergyman. Joyce and Edward would settle in California. Meanwhile, Dorothy married Ron Pike, a former neighbour of ours in Winnipeg, and they started their life together in Calgary.

My responsibilities with the CPR gradually extended coast to coast — and another change loomed. Midway through the 1950s, it was rumoured that I was going to become the CPR's system rules supervisor for all of Canada. Everybody seemed to know it before I did. When I finally received the promotion, I was a very proud man indeed. I appreciated the trust that management bestowed upon me. However, the promotion required that I move to Montreal — and Margaret wasn't sure that she wanted to go there. The CPR's chief of transportation came to see her and Margaret kind of laid down the law on him a bit. She loved her home in Winnipeg. She also had some reservations about leaving her friends. Her family was there too.

Margaret was the eldest of three daughters. She had a sister, Jean, fifteen years younger than she was. She was a secretary for a group of lawyers. Marge's other sister Dody worked for James Richards and Sons Farms in Winnipeg. She was the manager's secretary. She was very well known. Her husband was Irving Plumm. He was a cellist. He played with the Jasper Park Lodge Orchestra and in such places as the

Royal Alex Hotel in Winnipeg. Our fathers had passed away but our mothers were still alive, and she felt she had a duty to her family.

It was a question of moving to Montreal or not getting the job. My assignment was to re-write the entire CPR operating rules manual. I gave a lot of my life to the CPR. I was totally immersed in everything I did. It was a passion. The move was for our future's sake. You can't turn down a promotion. It doesn't come to every person to be asked if they want a certain position. Senior administrators would have filled the job with someone else but they courted me for it because I had such success on the western line.

When Margaret found out the promotion would considerably enhance my pension, she became more agreeable to the idea. We decided that she would come with me. If I had stayed in Winnipeg, I would have had to stay on the road, frequently inspecting stations in western Canada. Once she realized that I wouldn't be on the road as much if we were living in Montreal, she became quite ecstatic about the move. It was a very amicable arrangement.

She came with me immediately. She made a lovely home for us in Montreal. Our decision proved to be very wise to go because some things happened. For instance, Jean and her husband moved to Vancouver. I got train passes for her mother and my mother, so we enjoyed many happy visits. Margaret rode the rails with me as I examined all train operations personnel from coast to coast and we visited family wherever they were — in Winnipeg, Regina, Vancouver and other locations.

I had an instruction car that went over the whole CPR system, from St. John, New Brunswick to Victoria, B.C. It was self-contained in every way. I slept many nights in that car. Sometimes Margaret stayed with me but we usually went to a CPR hotel.

As I neared the end of my career, my primary task in Montreal was to help re-write the entire railway safety rulebook for all of Canada. I was the Canadian Pacific representative for the revision of the rules. I worked in conjunction with Canadian National Railway dispatcher

Neil Eckel and CNR vice-president Fred Somerton. The CPR asked me to remain for a year or two beyond my retirement until the new rule-book was completed, but we completed it in six months. (The extra service didn't count towards my pension.) Margaret wasn't very happy about me staying on — not at all. She was tired of the excessive travel coast to coast. She gave me a lot of inspiration and when I retired, we each decided that we would have our say about it.

Thinking back on these years, from my marriage to my retirement, I have to acknowledge Margaret's wonderful co-operation. I think I sometimes neglected my family but Margaret put up with me and gave me great inspiration. I was completely devoted to my work and had ambitions for promotion in which she upheld me. She gave me great inspiration to succeed. I was in the CPR for life. She gave up a lot of her home life to be with me as we travelled across the country as part of my job. It wouldn't have been possible to do what I did without her guidance. The theme, above all, was love. It would continue as I entered the next phase of my life. Retirement.

6

My Happy Retirement

Today many people fear the end of their Canada Pension Plan. Well, I've never had one. When I retired in 1963, the national pension program wasn't born yet. I didn't qualify for the Canada Pension Plan, introduced in 1966, because I had already completed my fifty years of work. I have successfully managed without the CPP now for almost forty years. (The federal government is probably glad too. Think of all the money that it would have had to pay me!)

Actually, my income is barely above the poverty line — about $1,400 per month. In over thirty-five years of retirement, my Canadian Pacific Railway pension has increased incrementally but has not yet doubled. Yet, my retirement has been beyond anything I ever dreamed of. I really couldn't have asked for anything better. I live on a fixed income, supplemented by my investments, but I have no debts or financial worries. I'm comfortable and I can sleep at night.

Simply put, peace and tranquility reign in my life. Believe me, it's nice to know at an advanced age that you can live comfortably. How did I achieve this blissful state? My retirement began with a plan. The transition to a new life should take place before you finish working. Remember, financial worries become a health problem. Choose safety ahead of speculation because fear of destitution can destroy you. You lose your morale and that spells the loss of desire to continue living in some cases.

Long before my last day with the CPR, Margaret and I sat down and decided how, and where, we wanted to spend our golden years. We

thought first and foremost of finances. I recognized it was necessary to prepare for cheaper money. In other words, you have to have savings to counter the rising cost of living. We also strived for good living conditions and a high quality of life. We sacrificed a great deal, eating at home instead of in restaurants or reducing our vacation travel, and we did everything ourselves rather than paying others to do them. We made things and we learned how to do our own repairs inside and outside the home. For instance, I did the paint jobs myself. We also used our garden to great effect, growing fresh fruits and vegetables. Margaret was great at preserving food and I still make crabapple jelly from her recipe and store it in a cool area in my basement.

We also made a lot of our own entertainment. We held parties and dances in our home and played bridge regularly. I still strive to entertain myself. I couldn't afford to pay $45 or more to go to a National Hockey League game. I'd rather go watch kids on the playground or outdoor rinks.

It might sound hard to believe but those early days of scrimping and saving, were the best times of our lives. They taught us frugality and, at the same time, we learned that money is not the only thing in life — just a necessity. Our life was built around family and friends and, although Margaret is gone now, that's still the way it is for me today. I just told you that my monthly income is barely above the poverty line. I have also tucked away a few dollars in interest-bearing investments. I haven't touched the principle of these investments which, are in the form of guaranteed investment certificates, and I haven't put more money in them (thankfully, because their interest rates aren't to my liking.).

I hesitate to go in the stock market with my savings. It's a risky business. Some people, like my brother, Wally, know exactly what they're doing and can take risks. I don't feel as comfortable and steer clear of the bulls and the bears that cause the market to fluctuate. I may be losing a lot of money but I don't lose any sleep at night! In my view, if you start worrying about the market you'll go nuts. Touch wood

because, so far, I haven't had to withdraw from my reserve. It's available in the event of emergencies — and they always come.

We prepared for unforeseen disasters by budgeting right down to the last penny. This detailed planning has worked out very well. My wants are minimal. The house is paid for. I don't have the cash to buy a new car — but I don't need one. Hopefully, I'll never need to rely on my investments and I'll pass this money on to my children, grandchildren, and great-grandchildren.

When Margaret died, she left her estate, derived from long-term investments, to the children. "You can have the house, Tom," she said. "Give the kids the money." My reserve money still serves a purpose for me, though. It gives me great confidence and peace of mind that, if I have to draw on it, I'll be able to have the same quality of life that I have now. If you're a senior citizen and want to leave an estate, take the long-term approach to investing — but don't deny yourself.

An early start to retirement planning is vital because a person's average period of employment is getting shorter all the time. I retired when I was sixty-five but many people today are retiring at fifty-five or earlier; and, retirement periods are lengthening as people adopt healthier habits and live longer.

You have to prepare for longevity. Take it from me, you may live a lot longer than other people including, as I have somewhat sadly discovered, younger members of your family.

Let me give you some retrospectives demonstrating how long you might expect to be retired. My next-door neighbor, Bruce Spies, retired recently and I went to his retirement party. Bruce was an instructor in the cooking program at the Southern Alberta Institute of Technology, a college here in Calgary. He went to work the same month that I retired — in 1963. I've been on the loose all the time that my neighbour has worked! According to Statistics Canada, four million three hundred and ninety-nine thousand two hundred Canadians will turn sixty-five by the year 2006. By 2030, the number of seniors is expected to jump to almost nine million. Who's to say that you're not going to live to be

100? In the United States, the number of people living to and beyond the century mark has tripled since 1980. In fact, according to the San Francisco Examiner and Chronicle's Parade Magazine, our age group is growing faster than any other in the U.S. or the industrialized world.

From day one of your employment period, it is a good idea to start saving on a very small scale. I gave Marge grocery money each month. In the 1920s, she invested $5 of that money every month for ten years in a retirement fund. Meanwhile, I put ten dollars per month in a fund of my own. By the time we retired, Marge's fund increased to five thousand dollars and my fund grew to ten thousand dollars. That reserve has been building ever since. We always paid our debts immediately.

As you get older, if you still live in your own home and rely on CPP and Old Age Security, you have to contain your expenses to meet your demands. I pay my taxes monthly through automatic withdrawal. I feel comfortable doing it that way because I don't have to worry each month. I also submit post-dated cheques to cover some other expenses. I spend about $140 on taxes, $65 on city water, electric and sewer services and $60 on natural gas. I've got my costs under control. There might be an emergency — a broken water tank, for example — but I can handle it. This careful, disciplined saving program has enabled me to enjoy financial freedom.

My primary concern at the outset of my retirement was to ensure our home would be mortgage-free. During the final five or six years of my career, sticking to the habits I had started much earlier in life, I saved as much of my earnings as I possibly could. When the time came, I paid $45,000 — in cash — for our retirement haven. My attitude toward retirement also helped pave the way financially. I like everything I do and that way it becomes a pleasurable deal. The goals of my retirement were, and still are, relatively simple: happy living, contentment, helping others, being close to family and assisting them when necessary. I set these goals a long time ago, but I still strive to realize them — every day. Remember: If it's going to be, it's up to me! And: You have to

believe it to achieve it!

I looked forward to my retirement. You really have to have a strong, optimistic outlook. Your retirement is the culmination of your life's work and this is the reward. You have to find it within yourself — and we did. When the time came, I embarked on my retirement with great joy and abandon. It was part of my life's plan. You can't work forever. Although I would have liked to, Margaret wasn't very fussy about that. Along with her, I made plans for living the rest of my life. It's essential that you think of your retirement as a new career. Margaret and I planned our post-railroad life that way. You have to school yourself and continue to drive towards success. Your retirement is really a full-time job and a full-time responsibility. You need to be self-reliant. You never want to be a burden on anybody. Drive yourself to capacity. Look for means of bettering your situation. Do things and do them well. Be proud of your accomplishments — very proud. You have to look for places to put your energy. You have a purpose and the purpose, mostly, is to give pleasure to others and to take pleasure for yourself. Choose a friendly atmosphere and a program of friendship. There's never a dull day in my life.

Focus on your family and how you can best serve their needs while still enjoying a busy, active life of your own. We planned our new life about ten years before I retired. I'd been through two wars and I was ready for some home life. It became quite clear that we wanted to be closer to our family. We had to decide between staying in Canada or moving south to the United States.

After Marge and I discussed the situation, that choice also became quite clear. Oh Canada! Or for our French-Canadian friends, Vive Canada! I didn't want to lose my Canadian citizenship because it has always meant everything to me. I fought for Canada in two wars and I'm extremely proud of my Canadian heritage. Canada was our home and it was familiar. We could still visit our family in California.

The financial world in Canada is geared more to senior citizens. Financially, I couldn't move to the States. I didn't have the means to do

it — especially today when the loonie is worth thirty to forty cents less than the U.S. buck.

Western Canada is a haven for retired people. There are so many things that we can do, so many things that are open for senior citizens. We can enjoy the mountains, the forests, the playgrounds, the golf courses and streams, so much open sky. (As I'm telling you this, I'm sitting in my kitchen area on a Saturday morning, looking out the patio window at my backyard and a small park. There isn't a cloud in the crystal blue sky.)

Now that we had decided to stay in, as the national anthem says, our home and native land, our children and grandchildren were still thousands of miles (or kilometres) away. We had to move west from Montreal but where to? Winnipeg, where our daughters had spent most of their childhoods, no longer held our dear ones. Our many trips to Calgary, home to our daughter Dorothy and son-in-law Ron, had been the highlights of our life and we thought the province of Alberta seemed the logical place for our retirement home.

Some of our closest friends had also elected to make their home in Calgary. With Dorothy and Ron's urging, it seemed the perfect place to start our new life. Everything was here — a little better weather than in Winnipeg and sports that fitted my plan. Hunting, fishing, and golfing were all available here. Sometimes I think it's a mistake to live away from my other loved ones but their distance gives you an excuse — and a pleasurable one at that — to see the world. Today's travel, thanks to the advances in the airline industry, isn't very far for anybody.

We made our decision in the late 1950s. We were living in Montreal and I knew that I would spend the last five or six years of my career in Quebec's largest "ville." As the CPR's systems rules supervisor, my primary duty was to revise and edit a new uniform code of operating rules governing all railways in Canada, including U.S. railways that operated in Canadian territory or on Canadian track. Everything under the authority of the Canadian Board of Transportation Commission was to be reviewed. For nearly three years, we had intensive study classes

reviewing all phases of train operation from our own system and some new innovations from the United States used on the New York Central, the Great Northern, the Northern Pacific, the Southern Pacific and the Chicago Burlington. All of these railroads were moving to the direction of automatic block signals and centralized traffic control to improve speed and safety.

Better and safer conditions were imperative to compete with other

CPR CEREMONY: In the fall of 1996, just before my 100th birthday, I attended a welcoming party as the CPR officially moved its head office from Montreal to Calgary. Behind me is an 1887 locomotive on permanent display outside Gulf Canada Square. I have fond memories of my days with the railway. Calgary Herald Photo

modes of transportation of goods and services, particularly trucks on super highways. Senior executives in the transportation departments of the two major railways, the CPR and Canadian National, assessed our methods daily. We had some disagreements but the skills and experience of all participants were mutually respected and we were able to produce a splendid new edition of operating rules. This included plans for greatly improved signal and radio equipment installation. The rulebook took effect October 8th, 1962. Many progressive ideas actually enhanced the longevity of this edition, and its merits survived until

January 16th, 1990, when computers and train dispatcher telephone communications proved their worth to make speedy and safer train movement possible.

We enjoyed some very happy times in Montreal, made many friends through the company and golf and curling associations. There was very little national disunity shown in those days and our social life included some fine families who had lived in Quebec for many years. I was pleased to receive a personal call from the chairman of the board of the transportation commission. He invited me to visit him in Ottawa, thanked me personally and suggested I become a member of his board after retirement. This was a great compliment indeed.

However, any further place in the workforce was not the wish of a lady ready to return to her home in the west. I was convinced that it was time to think of our retirement plans. I was on the road often during those Montreal years, visiting CPR stations across Canada. As my work came to completion, I periodically stopped in at Calgary and explored the construction of what truly would become our dream home. We contracted with a Calgary builder to design and complete our new home at 431 Wildwood Drive S.W.

We left Montreal with good feelings of a job well done, satisfaction in making such fine friends, having wonderful relations with the work-force and grateful to have lived in that beautiful city. It was a pleasure to know it and the people. I think it gave us great understanding of French-Canadians' just pride in their culture. We could never want any separation from the unique province of Quebec, nor from their resi-dents. It is an integral part of Canada that I trust and hope will forever be within the dominion. All of us would be diminished through separa-tion.

Before we left, the transportation staff in Montreal gave me an out-standing gift that has brightened many hours in my retirement days. This was a turning lathe and tools for fashioning all kinds of wood-work. I have used that equipment with pleasure and growing skill up until the present. Our new home on Wildwood Drive was near Dorothy

and Ron's former home on Grovehill Road and on the very edge of Edworthy Park, just below a famous Calgary landmark known as Broadcast Hill on which TV station CFCN and its radio affiliates sit. The park was named after Mr. George Edworthy, a well known pioneer and Calgary businessman, who donated the beautifully wooded land, located on the Bow River, to the city.

I was immensely pleased and honoured when Mr. Edworthy and his wife chose the lot next to ours to build their retirement home. He was a splendid and really wonderful man. He was also a generous, friendly and gracious neighbour, and so was his wife, until his untimely and sudden passing after only a few years of leisure living. That was a blow to all who knew and respected him, as well as to the City of Calgary.

Our Wildwood home and garden was everything we had desired. I had a workroom in which to store and use my wonderful tools and there was a large light kitchen, spacious living and dining rooms, and three bedrooms. Shortly after we moved in, I built an enclosed porch room at the back for cool summer evenings. Our back garden was large with lots of room for a vegetable garden and flowers and the view was enviable, for it overlooked a running river in the park below. Marge, as always, had such good ideas for arrangement of furnishings and chose such attractive colors and fabrics that the finished home was a joy to everyone who came.

We bought a new piano. It was Marge's choice and she happily used it every day.

I began to work immediately with my splendid lathe and tools and turned out, in the beginning, candlesticks, picture frames and bookshelves. Both our daughters were the recipients of these items. They were very pleased. I still see them in their homes today. As I became more skilled, I graduated to fine pieces of furniture: mahogany headboards, a cedar chest with drawers and writing desks for my grandchildren. Lamp tables and side tables with intricate edging followed.

Marge and I joined the Mayview Golf and Country Club, a new golf course on the then western edge of Calgary's city limits and within a

ten-minute drive from our Wildwood home. We golfed together often and met great new friends. Tom Milligan was one that I still hear from. On that street too, we grew to know the Fultons, Mel and Lila, and I guess it was fate because they became the dearest and closest friends of our lives. We played bridge together, went on trips together and even shopped together.

Later, we all belonged to the Turner Valley Golf Club, of which I am now a proud lifetime member. We joined Scarboro United Church and made more lifetime friends.

When you retire (if you haven't already), you'll find that your grandchildren become the focus of your life. In my opinion, all good things in life are contained in relationships between grandparents and grandchildren. I have always tried to encourage my grandchildren in everything they do and, as I continue to advance in age, they tell me that I inspire them with my positive attitude and many interests. Meanwhile, they help me stay young and in tune with the world. They also share my views on the advantages of maintaining good health, good habits and an optimistic outlook. It has been a great privilege to share birthday parties, other celebrations, and holidays with them. I keep very interested in their lives and try to participate in activities with them as often as possible.

My grandchildren and great-grandchildren live great distances away from me, in Nova Scotia, the Yukon, California and the eastern United States, but we say close to each other by exchanging letters, photos, and snapshots regularly. I am delighted whenever I receive their letters, art, or written articles.

By the time Marge and I settled in Calgary, we had five beautiful grandchildren to love and enjoy. Our first grandchild, Joyce's eldest daughter, Dorothy Anne Worthington, who goes by her middle name, was born in Pittsburgh, Pa., followed by her sister Laurie Bell Worthington and brother Edward (Ned) Arthur Worthington, who were both born in California. Dorothy gave birth to John David Pike, who went by his middle name, and Margaret Agnes Pike before we arrived

and then, ten years later, we were there to welcome Nancy Ann Pike. (Sadly, David and Laurie have passed away. I'll tell you about those tragedies, and how I overcame them, in the next chapter.)

Margaret and I vowed that we would always be there for them. If they couldn't come to us, we would go to them. Joyce, Dorothy and our sons-in-law made it clear they wanted us to be very involved in their children's lives. We felt very much wanted and needed, which is an extremely satisfying feeling. We enjoyed many special times with Dorothy's family in Calgary and, despite living far away, maintained close ties with Joyce's clan in California.

As we began our retirement, we took regular trips to California to visit Joyce's family. We were taken on great trips to the city of San Francisco and down the peninsula to Monterey and nearby beaches at Santa Cruz and Half Moon Bay. Usually, I managed to golf at the Palo Alto Club or other public courses. Marge was quite content to be with Joyce and the children.

As time went by, they visited us almost every summer. Dorothy, Ron, my grandson David and granddaughter Margie and I all spent many summers at Kelowna where Ron's parents had retired. Joyce and Dorothy rented cabins at Cinnamon's Resort right on Lake Okanagan. Marge and I stayed with the Pikes.

What happy summer days! There was boating, swimming, some horseback riding, and dinners at Tinglings. In 1965, Ron's father died suddenly. Mrs. Pike stayed on in Kelowna for some years but her two sons urged her to make her home in Calgary. She did and became part of our social life. Everyone enjoyed those visits and we were always welcomed with open arms.

Our grandchildren made us proud and honoured us by seeking our advice as we witnessed many special events in our grandchildren's lives: Graduations, weddings, and the arrivals of their children. Some of my proudest moments came during my one hundredth birthday party when five grandchildren and six great-grandchildren celebrated with me at Heritage Park in Calgary.

If you ask me, grandparents have a special role to play in their grand-children's lives. We are not the main caregivers or disciplinarians, so we can offer a non-judgmental approach. My grandchildren know they have my attention — and unconditional love. I want them to see and understand that they have a family heritage, a solid base that can always help them get through difficult times. I hope they will remember, and speak of, this ongoing heritage with pride — and rely on it for strength to carry on under any circumstances. My grandchildren and I gain security from each other, knowing we will always help each other. We have built a bridge which forever links us to one another.

Your grandchildren also help you gain an even greater pride in your home when you retire. We lived on Wildwood Drive until the summer of 1973 but, for some mysterious reason, we moved to an apartment on 90th Avenue S.W., much closer to Dorothy and Ron's place and very convenient to Chinook Shopping Centre. It was attractive and had a pool on the ground floor which we thought we would use — but did not.

In less than a year's time, we started to look for a home with space for a garden and a real backyard. We really made a mistake in that move from our dream home but decided to start all over again. We were fortunate to find a charming three-bedroom home in Oakridge where I still live today. We got to work, improved the property, decorated the inside and outside and had a lovely home once more. To our joy, the Fultons moved to Oakridge too and we resumed our close friendship.

I hope reading about the early days of my retirement will inspire you to plan ahead and adopt some of the habits and interests which I have benefitted from immensely. It's vital to keep up your social, sporting and other activities. After you've officially retired, you might also want to consider a new job, either full-time or part-time. (My daughter Joyce, who's in her seventies, has retired from teaching but still works as a receptionist. That job helped her qualify for U.S. social security, which American government jobs do not provide.)

Many people retiring today are just at the peak of their experience

and abilities. Companies can — and still do — benefit from their expertise. If you don't want to work for a living anymore, volunteer your services. I do a lot of things for people and they do a lot of things for me. I frequently speak to school children and seniors groups and gain a great deal of pleasure from knowing that, at my age, I can still help others. Don't lose touch with people just because you've stopped working. Continue to give what you can. I have a deep respect for people who are in ill health and continue to help. I give pretty generously to

CELEBRATION TIME: Marge and I pose during our grand-daughter Laurie's Wedding at Los Altos, California in June 1981.

Spear Family Photo

a lot of organizations, including charitable and health groups like the Red Cross, the Canadian Cancer Society, the Heart and Stroke Foundation, and the Alzheimer's Society of Calgary.

When I retired, Margaret and I, along with Mel and Lila Fulton,

joined the Southwood Seniors. It had about thirty-five members at the time but has now blossomed to about one hundred and fifty. We still meet every Thursday for lunch, entertainment and renewing friendships.

Often there is music and dancing, interesting speakers and countless celebrations. Every third week, we have a potluck lunch. This group has certainly made a difference in my life. Everyone there is kind and generous. More loving and caring friends would be difficult to find.

A FLOWER FOR MARGE: I present a flower to Marge on our 65th wedding anniversary on Sept. 17, 1986 during a party in the backyard of Dorothy and Ron's former home in the Lake Bonavista area in Calgary. The party was just one of many celebrations Margaret and I enjoyed after I retired.

Spear Family Photo

Don't be fazed by what you might consider a setback or a disappointment. A year after we moved to Calgary there was an ad in the Calgary Herald for a city traffic control administrator. I submitted my qualifications and received a brochure telling me my application had been accepted. But later city officials sent me another letter saying I was sixty-five years old and they hadn't recognized that. I didn't get the

job. I felt pretty bad about it at the time because I was keen to keep on working. But I directed my interests to other things and I've never looked back.

Moving into my current home from the apartment was also a challenge because we had to start all over again. But now I think this place is actually better suited to my needs than our dream home was. I'm closer to Dorothy and Ron's new home and I live within walking distance of medical and shopping amenities.

Don't fret about the end of your career either. Reflect on the contributions that you have made and continue to celebrate them. Nobody can take them away from you. In my case, once a railroader always a railroader. It's a funny thing because, now in my fourth decade of retirement, I don't feel out of the swing at all. Every time there's an accident on the rails — anywhere — I have to find out what's going on. My interest is still very keen. Keep in touch with your old colleagues. A visit, or even a telephone call, is a marvelous thing.

It's also very necessary to keep up with the world's daily events. Read the papers, listen to the radio, and watch television. These activities enhance your scope of living. I read the newspaper pretty well through. Any books I read are educational — and I read a lot of books. I like to have a picture of the whole world in my head so that, if anything happens, I can place myself there. I've discovered that, if you're geographically minded, you can visualize a place. It increases your outlook on life and gives you a proper interest in people. You can relate to people's moods and their difficulties, see how they handle life and what your judgement would be. In addition to softening your views and helping you become compassionate, these activities give you a great sense of enjoyment because, as you meet people — of any age — you're able to communicate with them intelligently. Don't lose this vital ability!

I would also advocate keeping a journal and writing about the events in your life and how you feel about the things that are occurring around you. I've kept a journal now for more than thirty years. Each day, I

briefly summarize what I've done, describe the weather, and recall some of my feelings about certain incidents or people. I started in 1967 but I reached way back for my story. It gives me a great feeling of satisfaction that I've overcome so many obstacles and I'm in a state where I can feel secure, happy, contented, and open-minded.

It's also very important to keep up your correspondence. I have an immense number of pen pals all over the world. They're a great source of pleasure and I get a great deal of motivation from them. Know how your friendships are doing. You have to change with the times and appreciate what other people do. Remember, there will always be greater or lesser persons than yourself. It's a wonderful thing to share your successes and failures with others. Tell others about your joys and your sorrows.

If you strive to do some or all of these things, your retirement will be just as delightful as mine has been. You'll also get through some of life's greatest tragedies. Just like I did.

7

Overcoming Tragedy

Early in 1989, Marge's eyes began to give her trouble. Suddenly, it seemed, she was not seeing well at all. Many visits to eye specialists revealed that her eye trouble was caused by macular degeneration. Although she took every precaution, her eyesight steadily grew worse.

She heard of a specialist in Vancouver, a Dr. Harris, who had been successful in treating eye conditions among the elderly. We called our friend Dr. Chris Moore, who was an ophthalmologist, and asked his advice. He encouraged us to see Dr. Harris of whom he had heard much also. After tests and examination, Dr. Harris said that improvement was unlikely. This was a severe disappointment to Marge.

Mercifully, we stayed with Jean in Vancouver for this appointment. The day after the prognosis, Marge had a stroke. It was not severe, but she had to be taken to Lions Gate Hospital in North Vancouver. She had suffered a little paralysis on her side and was very disoriented. Joyce and Dorothy came immediately and stayed with her until she was well enough to travel.

Six days later, we reserved six rows in a Canadair jet and, with Margie on a stretcher in the care of a nurse, flew back to Calgary to her doctor and Rocky View Hospital, just a few blocks from our home. Despite her wishes to return home, she remained in the hospital for several weeks. When she was healthy enough to move back to our house, we had homecare providers for a short time, along with Dorothy and Joyce. Thanks to therapy sessions at the hospital and walks around our house and block, she regained much of her movement and was certainly improved in her outlook and interest.

(I cannot write this history without speaking of our great good fortune in finding an excellent physician upon our arrival in Calgary in 1962. He has attended to all of our medical needs, examinations and conferences. He has been our advisor and our friend. We have been exceptionally healthy, but when we have needed care and assistance, he has come to our aid immediately. He is Dr. Manfred Hackemann and this man exemplifies the true doctor, the physician who treats the person as well as the wound. We know he is one in a million. Dr. Hackemann arranged all Marge's hospital stays, monitored her every day, and gave me wise counsel. He never failed us once in all her times of convalescence.)

By 1991, Marge was up and doing a few things around the house. We were able to celebrate our seventieth wedding anniversary at home in our garden with family and friends. We retained a homecare professional for a while, but Marge really preferred the two of us coping on a daily basis. I learned to do many chores, and I was glad to do them. Dorothy, Ron and Joyce were with us often and we managed quite well. I was even learning to cook in a manner that was satisfactory to a lady with very high standards.

Then, in February of 1992, another stroke sent her to hospital again. From time to time, we had her home, where she loved to be, but she became so weak and ill that she had to return to the hospital. On March 28, 1992, with our family around her, she passed away. Margaret Bell Spear was laid to rest beside our dear grandson David in Queen's Park Cemetery in Calgary.

You don't think about the day of a loved one's passing until it's upon you. Margaret's death was the most sorrowful time in my life. You feel like you've lost the better part of yourself. For a time, like the song says, the loneliness was the hardest part. At one point, I spent four days in hospital suffering from dehydration. I had to re-discover my love for life. Looking back now, I think I actually prepared for Margaret's departure — but I still needed a lot of help.

I really give credit to my family and my seniors club. They really

embraced me. They made me feel so welcome. They showed great love and affection for Margaret and myself by making themselves available to do kind things. They would be with me often. Just sitting quietly beside me, they formed a great bond. They supported me in everything I did.

Dorothy, Ron, Joyce and Shig were tremendous. I got wonderful assistance from Dr. Hackemann, too. He stayed right with me to the end. He put his hand on my shoulder and said: "Think of the good times, Tom. Just forget the bad times." I'm very grateful for such good support from my family, friends and neighbours. It gives me a great sense of security and it certainly inspires me. I still had to acknowledge my emotions. My advice to you? Accept that death is part of life to start with. You have to have faith that you will overcome. Really believe in it. Don't let despondence set in. The world is still a good place to live. You can be happy in it.

Don't be ashamed of tears. They are not a sign of weakness; they're symbols of love and affection. I am not ashamed of tears. Sometimes it does you good to have a good cry. You also have to meld yourself with friends and accept their help lovingly. It's a necessity and you should take great joy in it. How can you take joy from sympathy? It strengthens the friendship and you should show your appreciation by accepting love and sincere attention. It brings out love and support. Believe me, it's pretty nice to be able to call somebody on the telephone or drop them a letter, pour out your heart, and know that you will receive strength from the support of others. Be more aware of people around you and grateful for all the personal help.

Always welcome friendship. Everybody is a friend. How do you keep your emotions in check? You have to discipline yourself. It's very necessary. If you think that you're hard done by, why, nobody can do anything for your lost loved one. Your friends and family can comfort you. Don't rebuff them. Encourage them. Make your recollections happy moments. All of your memories of your loved one should be really happy. Forget the bad times. Just think of the great times you had

together. Speak of those times with your friends and family.

It's nice to talk about the old times. Don't avoid them. Share your feelings on them. The times you spent with your loved one are all yours. Nobody can take them away from you. A death brings the family closer together. We talk a lot about the earlier days. The children like to talk about them too and we have good records — pictures.

After Marge's death, it was just the loneliness that bothered me a great deal. I missed her a great deal but I believed that I was getting help and the sorrow subsided into affection. I don't think I'll ever completely get over being without her. I missed coming home to her. From every activity that I had, she just wasn't here. That was the hardest part of all. When I'm out and active, I don't think so much about her not being here. When you come home and there's nobody there, it can be a terrible letdown, but I have come to the conclusion that I can come in here and feel as if she has been here. That coming home part is still difficult. I get realistic and just say to myself, "She's just not here but, if she were here, I'd get the welcome." The home welcomes me now. I developed the sense of her nearness and what she would expect of me — I've never lost that.

So many things remind me of her. I have embraced them and taken them into my life. This is the way it's going be. I'm happy. I've found it a pleasure to do what she wanted me to do. I'm not expecting her to come back but I'm just trying to make the best of what she preferred right now. I let those feelings govern me, that she is very close. I'm comfortable with that feeling — secure. I always thought, "Oh, she's coming back." I knew it was fantasy but now I know that she's right here — in my thoughts.

Margaret is still a great inspiration. I feel her presence very close to me. I have little conversations with her in my mind, asking how she would approach certain situations. It's not a fantasy. It's something that's within my being. She's still alive within me — very much so. We really haven't lost one another. She's uppermost in my mind in everything that I do. Our lives were so intertwined that I feel comfortable

and secure. She is just totally in my mind in a very happy sense. I'm greatly strengthened by her. There's nothing I do in the house that I don't think of what she would do. I sure wouldn't do anything that she wouldn't want me to do. Marge is a continuing inspiration. She's that close. It's very comforting to think of the wonderful time we had together. In my mind, I review things that have happened and our great times together as a family. I'm not living in the past — I'm just reviewing the past.

About a month before she died, I steeled myself to the realization that I would have to carry on without Margaret. I prayed for a reason to continue on in the good things that she had done and would have liked to continue.

Wonderful health really has to be taken into consideration but now I feel that I have enduring contentment, security and happiness. There's such a thing as courage too. You have to be courageous. I think you have to want to like yourself. You should have a real good friend anyway but I think you must be your own best friend. When you lose a spouse, you have to have great faith in your prayers and what you still wish to accomplish. Margaret and I will meet again later on, after I depart this earth, but life here still goes on. You never forget but you get to have contentment.

When you've reached contentment, you can live a good life. You can take happiness from the younger children and things that they do. You should inspire people with your way of life. I just happen to love everything I do. You can develop that. Don't let anything detract you from the joy and happiness you get from doing things well. Losing a partner gives you a realism that you still have to carry on. You can't live forever and neither can anybody else. You must understand that death is part of life and it's your duty to continue with the aid of your family. You have to discipline yourself to keep moving, keep physically active, and keep thinking actively. You have to motivate yourself because, as I discovered, life can still be pleasant and productive. You must be interested in as many things as you can possibly handle. Time will take care

of your grief. Take great pride in what you have accomplished. If you start sitting in a rocking chair and watching TV all day, you'll get lethargic. Eventually, you won't be able to compete. You must have real desire and love for the things that occur around you. Take a very deep interest in your family and encourage them. Always show a happy smile. (I know that Margaret would want me to be content and happy.)

You have to continue your life the best you can. When Phil Donahue learned that Cloyce Copley and I had lost our wives after more than 70 years of marriage, he exclaimed, "Wow! That's gotta be an adjustment." Well, I just took over and developed the skills that cover the situation. Marge's illness was a little preparation for this and I have improved and even enjoy the kitchen activities. I was always interested in everything Margaret did in the last three or four years of her life. I had a lot of household chores to do and I enjoyed doing them with her. She was a very good housekeeper as well as an excellent cook and I learned a great deal from her. (I think she was the most meticulous woman I ever knew.) It's been a very rewarding experience.

Keep busy and love what you do. Time passes very quickly when you're busy. I never lost my desire to continue and that's because my health was so good. I didn't have any disease of any kind that interfered with my activities. I didn't have any pain, so I kept up my relationships and social calendar. I felt there was a purpose for me to continue and I never lost that. I still think there's a purpose — mainly to inspire others — and I'm going to pursue it. I think I'm still important to my family. They take great pride in my accomplishments. I still have the desire to do things and do them well. There's always new things to do and explore. I take great joy in accomplishing them and derive great happiness. So can you. Avoid despondence. I don't think comparison to other people is a good vehicle for elderly people. We should try to develop a life of our own. It can be done with good health. We can still be helpful to young people. Now, I have achieved a state of enduring contentment.

Of course, I didn't reach this level of contentment overnight. My

diaries speak of many sad and lonely days after Margaret's passing. In addition to all the loving support I received, I also helped myself — through meditation. During meditation, your body rests as the positive thoughts strengthen your desire for activity. It's a very relaxing period and it's quite stimulating. It makes you feel quite humble. It also strengthens your dedication to good living as it strengthens your mind. Since the promotion of the trip to Vimy Ridge and the tremendous effect it's had on me, the tragedies that I've experienced have all entered into my mind. Knowing that I have overcome them gives me a great sense of security and happiness. That pilgrimage probably fulfilled a subconscious desire. As our day of departure got closer, and I continued to meditate, my return to France became an obsession. That desire may have been in the back of my mind. Returning to Europe didn't seem that important to me. I was a little concerned about how I could handle it. I never thought I would get the positive results that I did.

One gets a sense of euphoria from meditation. (It's your own best drug.) The high that you get is comparable to the thrill of a kiss or an intimate hug. The feelings are both physical and spiritual. Remember, you've got to eliminate stress and worry. If you continue to worry, you're going to get sick. I get a great deal of satisfaction by cleansing my own mind.

A clear conscience is a wonderful thing. I've made mistakes but I've profited from them and been forgiven. It's a soothing of the spirit. You can think very clearly when you've washed your mind of all guilt. I think we've all got self-incriminations. You might want to sit down and straighten things out with yourself. Meditation just stimulates sleep and helps you realize that, no matter what has made you sad, life can still be very rewarding. I began to meditate — very frequently — after Marge's death. Now, I think of Margaret and the sadness of parting and it turns to reality and the knowledge that she's free of pain. I learned Margaret's illness was intolerable. She just couldn't get better. Her sight was gone. It was very difficult to watch her deterioration.

Sometimes, I felt guilty. I asked myself: Why was I so healthy? Why didn't I do something? Looking back now, I realize she showed a remarkable attitude in her dying. It was inspiring. She just didn't want

WARM THOUGHTS: Meditating with photos, like this one of Margaret, helps me savour the love we shared for each other.
Dean Bicknell Photo

to be a burden. She still had her desire. That stays with me even today. I realized her death was for the best. You see people in hospital that are really dependent on everyone. It's somewhat of a terrifying picture, isn't it? I thought of wonderful days when she was able to do so many things gladly and unselfishly. To know that she's at rest is very satisfying and comforting. I vindicated myself. In my own mind, I knew I did the best I could.

These periods of meditation are actually life scenes. Meditation can return you to your youthful days. It just takes me back to the really wonderful life we had together and helps me revisit the eras of my youth. I'm not sure why but meditation just came to me. Perhaps some sermons or religious connotation and memories of Dad and Mother's way of handling adversity triggered it. I've always been kind of addicted to doing some meditation when I was fishing too. Perhaps it also carried over from those times. On the river, I would just let my mind take in the streams, the sky, the water, the air and the freedom. I would forget everything. (It wakes you up when you get a bite though, I'll tell you.)

This inner reflection gives you an appreciation for life. These periods of meditation really stay in my memory. I feel so fit to meet the challenges of the world. A person has to have things going pretty much their own way to do this. I can relive the good things that have happened in my life. It gives you a great deal of satisfaction and desire to live. Your attitude towards the world is just wonderful. It's full of peace, joy and happiness. Meditation can also help you make very good decisions. It does with me anyway.

Usually, just before meditation, I have done something useful. I may have just written a letter, made a phone call or given somebody support. It just erases anger and distress. My meditations usually occur naturally when I'm writing or just soliloquizing. Bad things never show up at all. I always have visions of the beauty and gentle things of life. It's extremely stimulating. It cleans the slate and offers a new start. It gives your mind more freedom to explore. It's always a very satisfying ending. It gives you encouragement and purpose, reminding you to contact people, share your life and good times with others. It can happen anytime, mostly when you're alone and feeling that you need some stimulation. The things that may have been troubling you in life — your worries — just seem to disappear and they don't come back. You put them to rest. You feel that you've been aggrieved and you're just into a new life. It's very simple for me to drop into one of those meditations. You just slide into it. The transition is very calm. It's extremely pleasurable. There's no stress. I have come to a point in my life where I have an enduring feeling of comfortable relaxation and turn to unselfishness.

Silent prayer, that's what this meditation really is. It's a real cleansing of the soul. Granted, achieving this state of contentment is easier said than done if you haven't meditated before.

Let me show you how you can meditate. Your attitude towards meditation should be very positive. You have to induce meditation by getting into the proper mood and being at peace with the world. At the end of the day, you might be a little tired but it's quite easy to move into a mood of great satisfaction. Place yourself in comfortable surroundings

where things are quiet and appealing, amid things in your home that have become very personal. You might want to have memorabilia, pictures of people, or keepsakes that evoke fond memories. I usually meditate at the desk where I do my writing. On the wall above it, there are several pictures of my grandchildren, an invitation to my one hundredth birthday, letters and other momentoes. Around the desk are several books on a wide range of subjects, including fishing and golf. You want to clear your mind of all obstructions. Don't have any loud distractions whatsoever. You can't meditate with the television or the radio on. You must have silence. Now that you're ready to let your mind float, sit in a comfortable chair and close your eyes. Just breathe normally. You have to be totally relaxed and your mind must be clear of all worry. You are about to have a real visit with your inner self. You might even tumble off to sleep. Either way, you will likely be in a state of semi-consciousness.

It will give you great strength. You may be overcome by some worrisome act or news, a bereavement or some sadness in your family. Let your mind take you back to your memories. Tell yourself that nothing can detract you from your journey back to happier times. Free your mind of all encumbrances. Just think of all the good things that have happened to you and your family, even those loved ones who are no longer with you. Think of how better off you are than people in many other countries. Compliment yourself for what you have achieved. Just let your mind take over and wander to the good things in your life, something that you've accomplished, something that you would like to share with others. You're reviewing yourself. Wash your mind of all negative thoughts and worries. Be proud of what you have. Just float into perfect peace. You don't have to keep your mind blank. You may think of something that just happened and how grateful you are for it and then your mind spins off in many different directions.

After twenty or thirty minutes, you'll gradually come out of your meditation or, perhaps, start to snooze. You feel a great sense of accomplishment. Meditation shows you that you have to have a friend and, I

believe, that you have to be honest with yourself. In other words, be your own best friend — because you never know when tragedy will test you.

On this page, you see a picture of me riding on the back of a motorcycle with my grandson

LIVING IN THE FAST LANE: I still fondly recall this ride with David in Calgary in 1973,w hen I was 76 years old. It was just one of the many special times we spent together.
Spear Family Photo

David Pike, Dorothy and Ron's son, here in Calgary. In June, of 1973, we had a memorable day. We started from their house on Lake Bonavista Drive and sped out onto Canyon Meadows Drive. We rode around for about forty-five minutes. I was quite comfortable. It was quite exciting. I was seventy-six years old and that was the first time I had ridden a motorcycle since the First World War. It was a good heavy machine, a Harley Davidson, I think. The ones we had in France were small twin-cylinder dirt bikes. It was quite a thrill to ride with my grandson. It appeared to me David was a pretty good driver. He was caught up with the motorcycle age. He was quite into it and I had lots of confidence in him. I was very proud of him. I went to their house for dinner that night, concluding a good day with family. That ride was just one of many thrills that David and I enjoyed together.

Ron, David and I loved to go hunting and fishing. Those were special times for the three of us as Marge and Dorothy usually stayed home. We hunted ducks and pheasants. David and I were good friends. He always said, "It's no fun without you, Gramps." He had just graduated from Strathcona-Tweedsmuir, a prestigious private high school south of Calgary and was preparing for university.

It was a period of great happiness within the family, but that motorbike ride proved to be one of the last thrills David and I enjoyed together. He met his fate on July 6, 1974. Ronnie and Dorothy were at the Calgary Stampede, a world famous exhibition which attracts hundreds of thousands of visitors from around the world each year. When they got home, a police car was in front of their house. They just called us on the telephone and said Marge and I were wanted right away. From their tone, we knew something had gone terribly wrong but they didn't say what had happened or who was involved. When we arrived, they were all just sitting in the parlour. "Is it Nancy!" I asked.

She was just a little girl then and you always think tragedy strikes the most innocent victims. "No," said Ronnie. "Dad, David has been killed." He was eighteen. I just fell down. I was overcome with grief. We learned that David was a passenger in the front seat of a friend's car that crashed into a guard rail on Sarcee Trail, just below Broadcast Hill. The friend walked away with minor injuries. Rescue crews had to take a blowtorch to the car to get David out. The road was wet and there were all kinds of weather factors involved, but I don't think liquor played a role. The police investigation revealed the car did a three hundred and sixty degree spin and was punctured by the end of a guard rail. Dorothy and Ron later learned the end of the guard rail was turned outward with a sharp edge exposed to the road. Today, the ends of most guard rails are turned downward. You rarely see an open-ended guard rail anymore. (Even today, I never pass a guard rail without thinking about David's accident. As I pass every guard rail, I look to see whether the end is turned downward.)

We knew David had had a brilliant future ahead of him. We tried to stay away from blame because he was blameless. We tried to be generous in our thoughts for the driver of the car. We showed a great deal of sympathy for him too. Ronnie and Dorothy were wonderful about that. (He came to visit me after the accident and we cried together.) Still, David's death was very dramatic and very hard on us. Everyone was devastated. It was a family tragedy, because David was young and we

thought his life was just starting. It was a terrible blow because our hopes for him were so high.

Some very rough times followed, for who will not question themselves and the times and one's faith under the circumstances? Marge and I gave Dorothy and Ron a great deal of attention. We offered our support by being close to them and enjoying picnics together and trips to the mountains. We grieved with them. Our whole family, including Joyce and her husband, tried to help one another by being very close and protective, cherishing those left and making it possible for Dorothy and Ron's daughters, Margie and Nancy, to resume their young lives, for they were so deeply affected too.

That first Christmas after David's death, the Calgary family and Joyce and Shig met in Vancouver. With my sister-in-law Jean and her family there, we tried to ease the pain. Our friends certainly showed a deep sympathy and gave us loving support too. That support continues to this day. Ronnie was a scout troop leader and David was in his pack. They were a very closely knit group in the area where they first lived in Calgary, over on Grovehill Road. (Many of those families of boys and girls are still great friends. They're part of the chain of love and affection. It is still very strong.) We certainly leaned a great deal on our church friends. We got great support both from Scarboro United Church, where Marge and I worshipped, and Dorothy and Ron's church, St. Matthews. The wife of the St. Matthews reverend was a paraplegic and her desire, and ability, to overcome adversity greatly inspired us.

In each case, the whole church just gathered around us. They showed immense sympathy and made several visitations. They melded together very closely. They brought in a lot of food and were extremely supportive of all of our activities. These great friends have never let their support subside to this day. They still talk about David. Their memories and kind comments provide a continuing bond. My faith and prayers enabled me to accept David's death. The bottom line, of course, was love. I also had hope for David in the hereafter.

We look at his passing realistically now. It must have been a terrible thing for the driver of the car to live with. He and David were great friends. I am overcome with sadness, but not with any hatred. The accident, quite possibly, might have saved many other lives. That's the way we all think of it. We can — and do — talk about David a lot. We're comfortable. We realize that it was an accident. His passing is very memorable and sad to this day, but we take great joy from the fact that we had him for eighteen years. The years have passed, quickly, but that dear person is enshrined in our hearts — forever. We cherish the memories of everything he did. David's death is something we will never completely get over. That loss can never be amended; it has saddened our hearts — because love is forever. He loved the mountains where he skied, the trails, and all the treasures that can be revealed. He was so sincere and genuine in his love and appreciation for us, his grandparents, and for his mother and father.

As I mentioned, David, Ron and I loved to hunt together, but neither his father nor I have taken our guns to the field since his death. David himself would have wished that we kept hunting but we just couldn't do it. That showed that he was the motivator of those trips. He was part of every expedition, the guy that really wanted to go. Hunting is one of those things that, because we miss him so much, is hard on us. Ronnie and I always talk about "how the kid would have liked to do this today."

"I think of it all the time, Dad," he replies. Yet, we carry on. The lesson from David's passing has proved to be priceless to our family. We all learned how precious life is — and just how much adversity can be overcome. Ron and Dorothy have a good life and devote so much attention to their daughters. They go great distances to see their daughters Nancy and Margaret and their families today, in Halifax and Whitehorse, respectively, and I am included in everything that they do. I'm very proud of them, of course.

My remembrances of David are very happy, recalling how much David gave to us. He provided real happiness and friendship. We still

honor his memory by thinking of the good times that we had together and enjoy them again in our minds. We effectively relive the happy times and speak of them too. Dorothy, Ron, and I honor David on the sixth of July every year. We're very careful about what we do but we get together. I always go to their place.

What should you do when a younger loved one passes away? Grief like that is expressed simply through a silent embrace. Let the tears flow. Let peace and love take over. These times of parting are just part of life. They strengthen your will — and your faith — for sure. We were all encouraged because we had known the boy for eighteen years. His death made us realize that everybody is vulnerable. The support we received from our friends after David's and Marge's deaths helped us give more of ourselves to others during times of distress. We received so much satisfaction from a good many people and we realized we can certainly give our good wishes to those who are in trouble.

I discovered that, when your affections and your concerns are acceptable to others, you get a great deal of satisfaction. The feeling is quite catching. Emotions are generously received and there's a great bond of friendship. Just by remembering what you've gone through, you can provide guidance and inspiration. In motor vehicle accidents or other unexpected tragedies, there are always incriminations and people to blame. Be kind in those times and sympathize with anybody who is responsible for any accident. He too has to have grief.

Some of these so called tragedies change you for the better. Helping other people is a marvelous way of keeping busy and keeping yourself in touch and feeling that you are really loved and wanted — even in tragic circumstances. In our seniors' club, we're beginning to lose our friends quite frequently now, but everyone who has lost someone finds great comfort from the group. You have to show your appreciation of others. Let them know in times of tragedy and bereavement that you care. It helps your soul and it also helps theirs. It's what life is all about.

How can you help? Family support and close contact are very important. It's pretty difficult to appease grief all at once. Affection is what

they want more than anything else. They also want patience and sympathy — even tears if necessary. Get right on the same wavelength right away. Share daily visitation and car rides. Keep those feeling the saddest active but, above all, show sympathy. Don't neglect them. Stay with them as long as necessary. If they want to talk about their lost loved one, that's okay. Don't drop the friendship. Even a phone call a day can help. In time, it will be greatly appreciated. Sometimes a little pat on the shoulder or handshake does marvels. If someone tells you they don't want help, say: "Well, just think it over and, if you're in need, I'll be here. I'll be right beside you. I'm sure that you will overcome."

Time is a great healer but make it a happy time. Communicate with those suffering from sorrow. Share your joys, your experiences, your successes, and your failures with somebody. Be sincere in what you say. There's a learning process. You understand that these things happen. The realization that they happen to everybody really softens your attitude. I think you become a gentler, more generous person, and you feel good about doing good. I really do. When I do something good for somebody, I really take great pleasure in it.

It gives me a great sense of respect at my age to continue to help people, even if it's just a happy word or conversation. You don't know what influence you have. I have found in my appearances at schools and meetings that I've gained a lot of respect for being able to do some of the things that I do. I take great joy from this respect and show that joy. I'm extremely happy when I go to talk to people about living. I've learned that I can give help to those in trouble; that I can pass on support, love and inspiration. It strengthens you — and your resolve to continue.

My resolve was tested again in the spring of 1997. About a month after the Vimy trip, in May, Ron and Dorothy packed up their motorhome and drove to Whitehorse to visit my granddaughter Margaret and her family. They were to be gone for a month and they were looking forward to a long, leisurely vacation. At 6 o'clock on

Thursday, May 29, Ron's brother Jack Pike and his wife Bev, my neighbour Matil Spies and her daughter Lisa came to my door. I knew right away that something terribly shocking must have happened. They informed me that my granddaughter Laurie, Joyce's daughter, had died suddenly in California.

She was forty-three and the single mother of a teenage daughter, Kate — my great-granddaughter. She probably died from a rare congenital heart ailment. It was likely passed down through her father, who died at the age of fifty-six from a massive heart attack. We realized that we couldn't do anything about her death, although doctors might have discovered her condition — if they had known about it.

I viewed her death as a particularly sad experience because Laurie was very fond of me. She always saw the happy side of life. I remember all the good times I had with Laurie. She was always the fun kid. She always found something happy and bright to say. She was very warm-hearted. Her death was very unexpected because we thought she was in perfect health. She had always been a good athlete. She played tennis and soccer and also did a lot of swimming. She loved many other sports and served as a tutor with the University of California Golden Bears football team while she was studying at Berkeley.

At the time of her death Laurie was the manager of a bookstore in San Francisco airport. She had previously been a senior librarian at Stanford University.

Jack, Bev, Matil and Lisa were very caring, affectionate and supportive. Their visitation with me was extremely comforting because they too have all been through tragedy. Some of them stayed until I retired for the night. I promised that I would call if I needed them. I went to bed early but broke into a sweat. I took an aspirin and Fisherman's Friend cough drop. When I woke up the next morning, I made a simple vow: Carry on! I did an interview with a New York-based magazine writer, who told me she was doing an article about aging. For an hour and a half, I talked about aging and attitude, positive thinking and some of the other topics already discussed in this

book. It was time to practice what I preach.

In the intervening days before our trip to California for Laurie's funeral, I cut the lawn, planted some flowers and worked hard; spoke to my brother, Wallace, in Winnipeg; dined and kept in touch with friends; and prepared for the trip to the U.S. as Dorothy and Ron hustled home from Whitehorse. One night, I tossed in bed all night, still stricken with grief, but told myself that I must not break up emotionally. I felt that I must not break faith and stay strong and capable to support all of our loved ones. I was one hundred years old at the time, but I never thought of staying home. I felt that I was required there to make the family complete. I felt it was necessary to go and give support — and I did.

I just offered silent loving attention. There was a lot of weeping and sorrow. Laurie's death brought back my own bereavement with Marge. (Of course, family members from California had come up for me at that time.) My sister-in-law Jean Norvell and niece Susan MacArthur also came from Vancouver. The service was held outdoors in near-tropical surroundings. My granddaughter Anne (Laurie's sister) led the service and introduced many of Laurie's friends, fellow scholars and contemporaries that shared many of her life's aspects and pursuits. Those who spoke gave very complimentary and affectionate testimonials, showing loving and sincere respect.

It was an extremely warm and sympathetic gathering of lifetime friends, relatives and admirers. Joyce and Shig organized the arrangements extremely well and printed a special program and memorial verse. Great love, admiration and respect dominated the remembrance of a beautiful, talented and beloved woman. I'll never forget the loving support expressed from all who knew her as a friend, acquaintance or relative.

A day later, just our family members gathered for the interment of Laurie's urn at a cemetery full of beauty and greenery. Several wreaths and flowers were laid and Joyce read a passage that, in itself, could only be termed as what religion is all about. They were the finest parts

of the Bible's teachings, expressed in beautiful language from God's heart. They were exceedingly brave words of love and forgiveness and a prayer for faith and understanding between all members of our family. They were an expression of strong family unity — forever.

We cast no blame but asked for forgiveness and total, loving, understanding to help us stand firmly and lovingly together in the face of such a tragic loss of such a beautiful young woman, who was loved so sincerely by so many.

It was an extremely emotional experience, one that I will never forget in terms of its significance and heart-touching realities. Meditation again stood me in a good way to understand what a splendid, gracious and intelligent life I have had with my two daughters. I was the oldest person present. That fact sustained me too. I held up. I wanted to be a symbol of strong support by showing that it is possible to overcome tragedy and sudden bereavement. I still feel my influence is a continuing source of pride. We have all accepted Laurie's death as a no-fault tragedy. Of course, we still have Kate — Laurie's daughter. She now lives in Providence, Rhode Island with her aunt. She's the survivor and she'll be well looked after. Joyce and Shig set up a wonderful scholarship program for her and her quality of life will be as good as we can make it. We have great hopes for her.

What you just read, about Laurie's death, was supposed to culminate this chapter, but tragedy struck unexpectedly again in the fall of 1998. My aforementioned son-in-law, Shig Aoyagi, Joyce's husband, came down with pneumonia and was hospitalized off and on. A few weeks later, doctors determined that he had cancer of the esophagus. Adding to the problem was that Shig, a former chain smoker, was breathing through only one lung. Six years earlier, he had the other one removed — also because of cancer. He underwent surgery but his condition soon became terminal. Shig passed away in Los Altos, California on October 19.

I lost a very kind son-in-law whom we all loved dearly. He and I were very close. I'll miss our fly-fishing excursions along the streams

of Alberta and remember him as an excellent escort during my trip to the eightieth anniversary of the Battle of Vimy Ridge. He was a man of great integrity and a highly respected father and protector of his adopted family, which included one son and two daughters, including Laurie. This gentleman filled our hearts with love and affection for twenty-four years. I felt that it would be best if I stayed home, because a birthday party at my seniors club, and another at my home, had been planned — and I didn't want to over-exert myself before the trip overseas.

Dorothy and Ron headed to California and, for one of the few times in my life, I celebrated my birthday without any family members present. It was a testing time because I was stricken with sadness over losing Shig. I was also used to celebrating my birthday with my family. (Hundreds of relatives had come to Calgary from across Canada and the United States for my hundredth birthday.) However, my faith in God, memories of my youthful upbringing, my positive attitude, and the love of family and friends again saw me through a crisis. My seniors club provided loving affection and support — and a great birthday party. My birthday happened to fall on a Thursday, our usual meeting day at the club. Everyone brought a bag lunch and, with over one hundred gathered together for the celebration, we danced the afternoon away.

Later, my neighbours Bruce and Matil Spies welcomed me into their home for a delicious dinner, one of the countless I have enjoyed over the years, and many other special friends came to my home bearing cards, gifts, cakes, cookies and best wishes.

Despite the tragedy of Shig's death, and the absence of my closest loved ones, I had a wonderful day. Meanwhile, Shig was being laid to rest in California, next to Laurie, his parents, and Joyce's first husband, Edward. In addition to Dorothy and Ron, my granddaughter Anne, who manages a palliative care facility in New Mexico, and grandson Ned and his family came to be with Joyce. Together with some of Shig's relatives, they honoured the Buddhist tradition of carrying a lighted incense taper to the gravesite and knelt and sent a wish, or prayer, to

Shig. As Joyce wrote in a letter to me: "It was a beautiful day and I felt very sad, but thought he would approve of my actions . . . Dorothy and Ron have been of great help to me. There is much to do here and they have made suggestions and given me physical help to make my life easier . . . I am so grateful."

It was the second tragedy to strike Joyce in about eighteen months but, the love, attention, and support she received this time — and previously — helped her prepare for the days ahead without Shig. Using one of my favourite expressions she concluded her letter: "I will heed many a lesson in how to live alone — and carry on!" The circumstances surrounding Shig's passing and my birthday accentuated the fact that we all need friends and family to share our special experiences and our tragedies. I will forever be grateful for the loving affection they displayed. Once again, tragedy cemented the bonds of family and friends more tightly as we communicated over the phone and through heartfelt letters. This support took a huge load off my mind. I again learned that, in times of tragedy, you have to set your mind at rest. That's the crux of it all.

Dealing with Laurie's and Shig's deaths made me feel that anything is possible, that we should be prepared to cope with unexpected tragedies with a strong heart and know that the support of family and friends can see us through. When I see the influence and the respect that I get, it strengthens my desire to hold up. I certainly prayed very hard to be able to show great emotion but I gained a lot of comfort.

Laurie's and Shig's deaths, like Margaret's and David's earlier, were just two more experiences of life. In both cases, the complete support of the family was very uplifting. The togetherness made it possible to overcome our sorrow. I realized again that death is something that's going to come to everyone. I have quietly and effectively conquered all of the tragedies that I've faced. I know I'm a better — and healthier — person because of them. They showed me that we're all vulnerable to death. (Maybe these hardships tell you to get cracking before you go.) We should accept the fact that death comes to everyone — sooner or

FAMILY TIES: The closeness I enjoy with my loved ones has helped me overcome many tragedies. Shig, top left, and Laurie, top, third from left will be forever be missed but my granddaughter Anne and grandson Ned, also in the top row, and daughter Joyce, seated next to me, will carry on.

later.

This is not the end. It's the beginning of a new life for yourself and the person who has passed away. In other words, I believe strongly in the hereafter.

8

Keeping Faith

What makes me tick? Since I was a very small child, my religion has been the benchmark of my life. As you can probably tell from previous chapters, it has continued to inspire me up to the present day. Growing up in Manitoba, my brothers and sister and I used to kneel beside our beds and say a prayer each night:

Jesus, tender shepherd hear me
Bless Thy little lamb tonight
Through the darkness be Thou with me
listen to my humble prayer,
Watch my sleep til morning light
All this day, Thy hand has led me
And I thank Thee for Thy care,
Thou has warmed and clothed
and fed me,
Listen to my humble prayer
If I should die before I wake,
I pray the Lord my soul to take
God bless all my family and all my friends.
Amen.

I still say the same prayer: My religion is the source of motivation in everything I do. Before I do anything, I consider right versus wrong. For me, in all my decision making, God comes first; my family comes

second; and my country comes third. My motto is: Take it to the Lord in prayer. That's the way I live my life. My return is hundredfold in satisfaction and love. My faith directs my being. It directs my acts.

The thought is the father to the act. The overall effect is abiding grace and happiness. In other words? A peaceful life. Remember how I told you how World War I changed my outlook forever? Well, it was my faith that pulled me through and gave me the inspiration to carry on. I just put my faith in God. We were subject to death at any time when we were in service. I believed in my faith and accepted whatever came along — including my brother Will's death. His passing was a very sobering moment that I've never forgotten. It was a turning point in my life. It was the basis of a new understanding, peaceful and sorrowful, but grateful to return home safely. This, what you might call epiphany, just grew on me in my normal living and my happiness. I valued my family. I became a great deal more unselfish. I found great pleasure in this awakening.

I attribute my success in my work to my attitude, which comes from my faith. It has been a great support for me all through my life. Pride and patriotism have never faded. Never. My faith keeps me active, motivates me, and gives me encouragement to do the things I like to do. This is all possible with good health, which was endowed by God. I get a lot of inspiration from Dr. Robert Schuler of Garden Grove, California, who hosts a weekly religious television show called This Hour of Power and has also written books designed to help people get the most out of life. He's a very positive minister of things that should be done to keep the world at peace. His sermons have motivated me a great deal and given me marvelous support.

Dr. Schuler's greeting every Sunday morning is: "This is the day the Lord hath given. Let us be glad and rejoice in it. Accept the fact that the Lord is with us and within us. Let Him direct our paths."

That's exactly how I feel. (That's what my dad always said, too. He was a great educator.) I would hope that you would try to set your path in the same direction. My faith has certainly enhanced my life. I'm sure

it will enhance anybody's life if they dedicate themselves to the ways of goodness and righteousness. My faith has made my life better. My faith in Him has allowed me to have faith in myself.

I pray for perfection in everything that I do. I think I've succeeded in most things, to my own way of thinking anyway. My faith is very strong. It's reasonable. I'm not asking for things that are out of my reach, because I feel that a person can accomplish anything if they have the faith and motivation to do it. My standards are high and my standards are motivated by faith. If you ask me, people of any age can maintain positive mannerisms, a high quality of life, and an appreciation for the good things in life. I have faith that they will continue.

I have to think about my faith. It's workable. If it's going to be, it's up to me, but the big thing is that I enjoy everything I do and I am proud of my accomplishments. I feel so badly when other people don't get anything out of living. I feel as if I should be doing more to help them.

As you can tell from some of the previous chapters on my public appearances, my war experiences and the tragedies which I have faced, my personal life has been rather unique. In times of trouble, I really take it to the Lord in prayer. I really do. That's meditation. It always seems to work out. When you avoid temptation, you have succeeded. There's always a substitute for temptation. You find that substitute through discipline. My faith is a natural law of necessity. I'm the kind of guy that is swayed with emotion and my faith helps me control myself. I have to have faith in my prayers because, deep within me, I know what I want to do and, if I have faith, I will nearly always succeed. Success will follow success. Your prayers have to be reasonable and realistic.

As the hymn says: It's no secret what God can do. What He's done for others, he can do for you. Somewhere in my life, probably in my dad's early teachings, I adopted that philosophy.

My dad's heart was in his service — it really was. He continued until his very last days spreading good tidings and great joy — and I strive

to do the same. In my opinion, you don't have to be an elected leader to be a leader. You can do it by virtue of maintaining high standards.

I hope I've succeeded in that at least. I believe in my faith and practice it daily at work, play and everything that I do. I rejoice in the day the Lord has made. There are many good things to do.

Your faith doesn't have to restrict your happiness. We were brought up in the teachings of the Bible but that had no restrictions on our happiness. However, we're not free. We're bound by personal law, by laws of nature. We have to learn to give in. Freedom has its bounds within the jurisdiction of personal relationships. My attitude, based on my faith, is very peaceful, forgiving and optimistic. My attitude grew and is still growing. I kept it growing with a very optimistic outlook.

Everyone gets the blues, including me. I just get positive every morning and have a little talk with myself. I just know that everything is going to be all right. How do I come across? As a braggart? I don't want to be boastful but I'm living proof of what can be accomplished. I just want you to see me as a happy centenarian offering information that's truthful, helpful and inspiring. I'm very humble and I'm thankful for that humility. I've entered into a state of continuous happiness. I'm sailing along very smoothly on the River of Life — and enjoying every day.

If your faith is strong and you let your heart flow out to it, you too can be a happy person. My standards are high and my faith in my standards really motivates me. This faith is wonderful, but the big thing is to enjoy everything that you do — and everyone you meet.

I was raised as a Christian but, in my heart, I'm non-denominational. Christians, Jews, Muslims or people of any other religious persuasions are all the same to me. They have equal status. They're part of God's great creation. My dad was the same way. It didn't matter whether someone was a Roman Catholic or a member of any other denomination. There is a divine being, whatever you perceive Him to be. The same principles are written for everybody. There are great religious differentials in the Bible. The people overcame. Everybody's

heart should be turned toward peace.

I live not only for myself but to please others — and help if I can. If I have the kind of faith and positive living that may help others, I hope I can convey that to good advantage. I'm beginning to think that's my role in the publishing of this book. I have great faith in it. I've received several nice letters about it. If I can help others carry on, my book can be my trademark.

FAMILY PHOTOS: Here, in my home in Calgary, I show some old photos to my great-grandchildren Nathan and Sara as they visit from Whitehorse.

Dean Bicknell Photo

My faith has shown me I've got to keep up my interest in life. I just can't sit back and let the world go by. Set your goals high. Take a real good try at everything you do.

I'm kind of living in euphoria. Somebody must be looking after me. I acknowledge that. If I could be an example to others questioning how their faith can help them, especially seniors, I would say I've always enjoyed life. It's just great to see the sun shine each morning. It's just terrific to be able to get out on the golf course and walk around, let alone play a pretty good game of golf. I don't flaunt my faith but I try to express it within my family.

My family's love and respect for me goes a long way in keeping me motivated and independent. A good family is a marvelous inspiration. Life starts there and continues there to the end. My family's health and

BRIDGING GENERATIONS: Dorothy, Ron, and I spend some quality time with their grandchildren, my great-grandchildren, left to right, Nathan, Carson, Sara and Kyle.
Spear Family Photo

welfare comprise my number one interest. They all enjoy a fine quality of life — exceptionally fine. That's what we all strive for.

Time goes by very quickly. I've aged with my children and grandchildren. I learn from them and strive to inspire, support and love them dearly. With my faith also comes desire. It's not the desire for power. It's the desire to succeed and develop happiness and friendliness in the world.

Onward and upward! I pray for the continuation of my desire. It's a very happy life. Share yours with others. My attitude, based on my faith, is the secret of living well. Everything is going to work out for the best. There's always desire in my heart to enjoy things as they come along. I kind of amaze myself with the things I can do at this age. I'm constantly tuned to my learning channel. In myself, I feel that I can contribute with my experiences. That's my greatest desire now. I just have to sit down and discipline myself and get into the mood of meditation, knowing that there's something better.

Trying to maintain my desire gets more pleasant all the time. This

desire is the secret of good living — happy living — and it creates a lot of vitality.

I try to maintain my faith in my daily living and everything that I do. I ask for ability and strength to carry out my desires. I never criticize anybody else. I correct myself. If I make mistakes, I profit by them. Thanks to my faith, I have a very flexible attitude towards others, and a splendid respect for everyone I know. My friends have shown me that prayer is all right but you have to have faith in it. One lady at our club is disabled because of a broken hip but she's active in her mind and gives full support to others. She has faith that she can continue. She doesn't want to be left out. She's willing to do her share. She still isn't able to do the things that she wants to do but she still tries. It costs her — in pain — to do them. Still, her face portrays the love she has for other people. She is a very delightful person. Realistically, she knows she is disabled but she is just making the best of her situation. She is not crying or showing any signs of giving up. She takes part in everything. She is admired by everybody. She used to be in a wheelchair but she got rid of that. She got a cane and walked. Sometimes she throws the cane away, but if she's in a crowd she keeps it with her. Her attitude is very positive. She does her part. She goes on trips. She visits a great deal. In her own disability, she's a role model. She used to come in her wheelchair to visit my wife Margaret in the hospital. This lady's outlook is exemplary. She must have a deep desire within her to do things and she accomplishes those things despite her disability. I have even seen her dancing.

Our faith should give us comfort. Having a similar attitude can do for anyone what it's done for me. It's quite possible to change your attitude into something that's pleasing to you. It makes for a very pleasant life. Health-wise, having a similar attitude will give you a feeling of freedom and a feeling that you are making the best out of life.

Other people from our seniors club have been very sick and they have placed their faith in their prayers. They have been rewarded with much better health. I'm sure faith will enhance anybody's life if they

dedicate themselves to excellence, goodness and righteousness. It's made my life peaceful, joyful and very rewarding. It influences everything I do. I don't let doubt shroud my objectives. My way of life has been very humble and rewarding, and has made my life pleasurable in all ways. I wish the same good fortune on everybody. As the Bible says: "Train up a child in a way he should go and when he is old he will not depart from it."

My faith motivates me, sustains me, and comforts me in every way. It becomes a way of life. I pray that I can retain all of those good things that come from a positive attitude. What fires up this attitude? Spirit. My soul is the governing prize. Our spirit, I think, is likely the conveyor of the good in us.

I was out for dinner with friends one Sunday night; they're quite religious people and the minister had spoken to them that morning about the soul and the spirit. They asked me what I thought. I told them about my nightly prayer: "If I should die before I wake, pray the Lord my soul to take." That feeling is something that's developed inside my soul. It's very precious. My spirit is the director. I think that there's always good living. As part of that good living, all those things — God, family, country, morality, honesty, integrity, discipline, a healthy lifestyle — are in my soul and my soul directs me. The spirit within me motivates me. If there's a very strong spirited animal like a horse, people talk about the great spirit in that animal and the same thing applies to the human race. The spirit is the ultimate power. You can cultivate that spirit. There are so many kinds of spirits, including the spirit of love and even, possibly, evil. You have to develop a personality of your own based on the Ten Commandments (or similar governing principles stated in different religious texts). In my view, you have to be good to yourself to live pleasantly. You have to make your life pleasant and happy and, if you do, all the good things in your life will be stored up in your soul, in the form of good thoughts.

I think then you'll have your life's direction — you really will. No matter how old you are.

9

Aging with Desire

As I told you at the beginning of this book, I still have my driver's license. My ability to drive at my age has become quite a novelty. I believe a lot of people didn't believe I could drive. You picture someone who's over one hundred and you imagine someone who is in a rocking chair or is not too well.

As mentioned earlier, when some U.S. television producers learned I still had my licence, they invited me to appear on their shows early in 1997. During my appearance on Donahue, I met Dr. Thomas Perls, an assistant professor of medicine at Harvard Medical School, and geriatrician at Beth Israel Deaconess Medical Center. Dr. Perls invited me, along with my "kid" brother Wallace, who celebrated his one hundredth birthday on March 30, 1999, to participate in the International Centenarian Sibling Pairs Study. This study, is being conducted in conjunction with the New England Centenarian Study, which covered

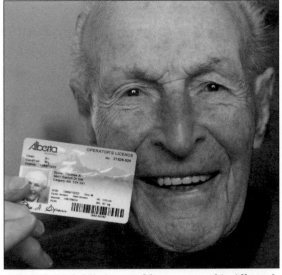

HERE'S PROOF: I was able to renew this Alberta's driver's license until at least October 22, 1999.
Dean Bicknell Photo

centenarians in the Boston area only. Dr. Perls is the founder and director of that study.

Wallace and I, along with other siblings, who are ninety- eight or older and ninety to ninety-seven, have provided tablespoonfuls of our blood to a Harvard research team led by Dr. Perls and Dr. Margery Silver. Using our blood, these researchers are attempting to identify genes which enable people to live to one hundred

DRIVING HOME: My Olds Cutlass Sierra takes me wherever I want to go. But on winter days like this one, in January of 1996, I don't go far.
Calgary Herald Photo

years of age or longer. It is hoped that their findings will eventually help prevent such diseases as Alzheimer's (which unfortunately claimed one of my closest friends), other forms of dementia, and arthritis — just to name a few — which are known to afflict the elderly.

"We have a hypothesis that centenarians represent the model for successful aging," Dr. Perls told co-author Monte Stewart, adding centenarians only suffer from major sickness late in life. "We have made the finding that they have lived the vast majority of their lives in excellent health."

Dr. Perls has already managed to disprove some theories — especially his own. "I was a fellow in training in gerontology and always had thought the older you got the sicker you got," recalled Dr. Perls. "I had these two patients who were (around) one hundred. One was one hundred and one and the other was one hundred — and I never saw them in their rooms. They were always out doing something. So I actu-

BLOOD BROTHERS: Harvard researchers hope Wallace's and my genes will help answer riddles about seniors' health woes.   Spear Family Photo

ally had to book an appointment to see them in their hospital rooms." In other words, the centenarians participating in the study, and quite likely future generations who reach the same age "are going to spend very little time in poor health."

Why is this information so important? Post-World War II baby boomers are on the verge of becoming senior citizens, generally defined as people sixty-five years of age or over. Statistics Canada forecasters predict that by the year 2030, half of Canada's population will be over forty-five and the sixty-five and over crowd will have grown twice as fast as the general population. Currently, more than two million seven hundred thousand Canadians are caring for someone with health problems, usually a senior relative. This huge seniors population boom is going to pose a major challenge for what is known as the sandwich generation — people who care for children and their aging parents. According to Statistics Canada, about eighty-five per cent of people in their forties have a living parent and dependent children. Since women tend to be the primary caregivers in families, they

will likely face the biggest demands in the years to come.

"It's going to be a very big issue," predicted Dr. Perls on the impending seniors explosion and its impact on the sandwich generation. "They're going to be looking over their shoulders while their parents are going to be needing a lot of care. They're going to be taking care of their kids as well as their parents."

Governments, health and social agencies are now trying to find new ways to care for seniors at home and other facilities than hospitals or nursing homes. According to Dr. Perls, many people believe that future centenarians are going to be a burden but he believes that learning why

BIRTHDAY BOY: I received this sweatshirt from my friends at Southwood Seniors Club for my 99th birthday. What an honour it was to be compared to now retired hockey star Wayne Gretzky.
Calgary Herald Photo

centenarians live so long might actually help ease the pressures of the forthcoming boom. The Harvard researchers, said Dr. Perls, want to learn how centenarians stay healthy for so long and try to see if any of that information can be translated into letting others — namely younger generations — do the same.

There's probably not going to be one "fountain of youth" gene but

Dr. Perls is confident his team will pinpoint approximately ten genes that promote longevity whereas it was previously expected there might be thousands of such genes. Dr. Perls and his team have already made some key discoveries. Just two centenarians in the study were diagnosed with cancer — one with breast cancer and one with pancreatic cancer.

CARDS GALORE: These are just some of the cards I received for my 100th birthday, on Oct. 22, 1996. When co-author Monte Stewart interviewed me about that birthday, he asked me what I planned to do in the future. I told him I would carry on. Calgary Herald Photo

"(Cancer) is a major killer of people, so here's a group that have escaped," noted Dr. Perls, adding cancer is a leading cause of death along with heart disease, stroke and dementia. Dr. Perls and other researchers have also discovered that genes linked to Alzheimer's disease, which tends to kill people in their eighties and early nineties, are not prevalent in centenarians.

In addition to analysing our blood, Dr. Perls, Dr. Silver and others in their research team have also interviewed us at length about our employment history, careers, families, and lifestyles.

"We haven't seen any patterns (i.e. definite answers) in terms of their

environment," Dr. Perls told Monte Stewart. "None of them are fat, really. None of them smoke. None of them have a history of cancer, although I can't say that about prostate."

The study also determined that centenarians come from all ethnic and racial backgrounds. Their financial situations range from poverty to huge wealth. Their education levels range from as low as Grade 2 to as high as doctorate degrees. These findings suggest that education, although it's known to help people live longer, and ethnic origin cannot pre-determine whether someone will live to be one hundred. However, the researchers have made some key, purely scientific, findings. Siblings in good health have a four times greater chance of living to their early nineties. Women who are now centenarians had a four times greater chance of having children after they reached forty years of age. Frail elderly women are also able to live with disease longer than men. For some still largely unknown reason, disease attacks men more viciously.

In other words, according to Dr. Perls, I am bucking that trend. "Obviously, he is a very incredible man," Dr. Perls told Monte. "To get to one hundred is amazing. He is obviously among the best centenarians in our group. For a man to get to his age, he has to be quite exceptional. In terms of his physical fitness, he is quite exceptional. The fact that he plays golf is quite remarkable."

Actually, shooting below my age gets easier with each passing year.

I also enjoy curling and fly fishing. (I spend many hours tying flies with a vice in my home.)

Guess what? I actually started participating in most of these sports during my childhood in Manitoba.

There wasn't too much entertainment in those years. We had to make it for ourselves. Three boys and a girl — my brothers Will, Wallace and our sister Helen and I — went to work at it. We made our own curling rinks and our own skating rinks on the Roseau River which ran by our home in Dominion City. We made the curling rings and dyed them red and blue with liquid dyes and dolled up our curling stones, which were

cut from logs. They were about a foot thick and a foot in diameter. They had ribbons and spikes which we used as handles. All our neighbours would join in. Each of our families had rinks on different parts of the river. We would also play hockey, clearing sheets of ice along the river and we used magazines for shin guards. We had wooden pucks. We just cut circular pieces about an inch and a half thick from the abundance of

COMPOSED CURLER: I still enjoy curling in my advanced years, although I'm inclined to limit my participation now because I don't want to risk injury. This photo was taken at the Calgary Seniors Curling Club, when I was 98 years old. Calgary Herald Photo

trees nearby. If we got a hockey stick for Christmas, we got a real Christmas present. A pair of skates lasted as long as the boots fit you. By creating these games and pieces of equipment, we became very independent.

We made virtually everything else that we needed. Our dad was a great innovator. He could make anything and he had the tools to do it. This love of sports has flowed all through my life, with great intensity. It never left me at any time. My brothers and sister developed the same passion for competition.

From the time I started work in 1912, I started competing in curling, hockey and baseball. I used to curl in the Manitoba playdowns. My

rinks competed against Morris, Dominion City, Letellier and other towns. One year, we won the Manitoba double-rink championships. Two rinks would compete against two other rinks in any other area and advance to the Manitoba championship.

Those curling rivalries flowed over into hockey. We took special trains to the respective towns in the play-offs. We would get three hundred people per game. The train trips were just happy parties. Emerson really dominated. We were a little larger

HOMETOWN HOCKEY: I started playing hockey as a boy in Manitoba. This photo was taken when I was about 12 years old. I'm still a big fan of the game. Spear Family Photo

town than the others. While playing relief goaltender, I took a puck in the mouth and lost a front tooth. The lighting in the rink was very poor. It was a long shot from centre ice and I couldn't see it. I looked more injured than I was, with my swollen face and mouth and lots of blood.

Marge was aghast and even Joyce, then just a baby, cried upon seeing me. We were fortunate to have a young Toronto-born dentist who was also our star hockey player. Dr. Dalton Boyd fixed things up with a peg tooth which filled the gap nicely. That tooth had a habit of coming out; corn on the cob was usually the big culprit.

The injury didn't stop me from playing though. One year, our Emerson team challenged for the Allen Cup, still the most coveted prize in amateur senior men's hockey today.

I can recall a fantastic series with Kenora. We played in the old Winnipeg Arena by the CNR station. Kenora beat us and eventually

BOYS OF SUMMER: Our Emerson baseball team attracted big crowds to games. Incidentially, I'm in the centre of this photo, taken in the 1920s, wearing the black sweater and cap.   Spear Family Photo

won the Allen Cup title. Kenora had a wonderful goaltender, Chuck Gardiner, who later went on to play for the Chicago Blackhawks between 1927-34. I used to see him when he went through Emerson on his way down to training camp. He was a classic playoff goaltender. His National Hockey League career regular season record was somewhat misleading — 112-152-52 — but he still posted 42 shutouts. In the playoffs, he sparkled with a 12-6-3 mark — there was no overtime in those days — and five goose eggs. He also helped Chicago win a Stanley Cup!

I never had any professional hockey aspirations because there was no pro team nearby. Those were the days of the NHL's original six. The league didn't expand until 1967 — when I was seventy-one years old.

In summer, I played catcher for Emerson's baseball squad. We played in the Ameri-Canuck League, comprised of our town, and the towns of St. Vincent, Pembina, Hallock, Drayton, Neche, and Grand

Forks in the U.S.

Emerson had two professional pitchers, a lefthander and a righthander. They were called barnstormers and we paid them one hundred dollars a month. We usually had pitchers who were professional ball players. They were young men in their twenties who shared the proceeds of tournament winnings and received one hundred dollars per month from the club. They came back to us year after year and, along with a couple of hometown boys, Charlie Unsworth and Archie Saunders, provided us with solid pitching. They allowed us to keep the Emerson Ball Club the pride of the league.

I loved every minute of being their catcher. One pitcher stands out as a winner, a semi-pro named Henke. He was a lefty and played in "Boomer" leagues that went from city to city. He returned to use for some years and his "ins", "outs", and "drops" now termed sliders, curves and fastballs ensured our team won regularly.

Marge and I made lifelong friendships through these activities as we travelled together and cheered our teams on. I drove some teammates to the different towns in my Hupmobile. About nine of us, sometimes with one of the umpires, would climb in. The town's butcher was a big fan. He had a Ford and he would take the rest of the team in his car. The hotel owners really deserve mention and praise for their loyalty because they provided food and lodging to keep good sports alive for the townsfolk — young and old. All housed "Boomer" ball players for pride of town and community.

There was no monetary incentive. Playing baseball cost us all money. We paid for our own gas and cars. There was no remuneration whatsoever. I just received great satisfaction — and pride of town. I was scouted by the American League's Chicago White Sox, but my love of home prevented me from going any further. I think I was capable of doing better but I didn't want to turn pro because I was too happily situated where I was with Margaret and our daughters Joyce and Dorothy.

Some people might say, what about the money? I wasn't interested.

You get all the satisfaction from within you. You've gone all the way if you've done your best.

Still, we followed Major League Baseball with a deep passion. I remember one time during the World Series when Babe Ruth came to bat. He pointed his bat to right field and he put the ball right there. I've always remembered that. There was no television then. The way we got baseball games was by telegraph — play by play. Every play, and comments, would come over the wire. In Winnipeg, the Free Press and the Tribune had big billboards on the sides of their buildings and crowds would come to see them. The Free Press and Tribune sportswriters served as the announcers. They had great announcers and they'd embellish a lot. The announcer called the plays with a big megaphone. It was pretty clever the way they described the pitcher and the windup.The announcer would get the plays off the wire. "Strike! Ball!" There was no TV and there was no communication by telephone.

Meanwhile, from my train station in Emerson, I intercepted messages being dispatched from the city where the game was being played to the Free Press. The games were played in the afternoon and my telegraph office waiting room would be full of guys waiting to know the plays. I would copy the information with a manual typewriter and just hand slips of paper to the guys. For four or five years, the Yankees and Giants played each other. It was a great rivalry. Most of us cheered for the Yankees. The stars — Ruth, Lou Gehrig, Yogi Berra and others — appealed to us. We used to have pools predicting the final score. Fifteen or twenty participated. We drew the score out of a hat. The winner had to have the actual score or be the closest to it.

We didn't have radio. In the 1920s, a crystal set came in. That was the first radio we ever had. It wasn't all that clear, but it was voice. You had to listen to it with a headset on. We'd get together in the station. The headset wasn't very reliable. The crystal had to be adjusted from time to time. We usually went to the telegraph.

The first — and only — live major league game I ever saw in a stadium was in Pittsburgh. We went down to visit our first grandchild,

Anne Worthington. It was quite an experience. Hank Greenberg had a sign up in left field. That's where he usually hit his homers. The Pirates were playing the New York Giants. That was pretty big stuff for a kid from Emerson to go to a National League game. I remember I got a couple of programs and sent them back to my hometown. I was alone. I stayed there for a doubleheader, all day with my own lunch. It was a thrill.

My early love for sports, and desire to excel, helped me prosper in golf, which I didn't take up until the relatively late age of thirty-nine, after I stopped playing baseball. In the 1930s, as interest in the sport started growing, other Emerson sports enthusiasts and I founded the town's golf club and set out to build a course. We located some farm-land about a mile north of the town on Highway 75. We rented that plot, less than one hundred acres, and our volunteer crew cut, levelled and laid out nine holes. The course wasn't long but it was difficult and we sharpened our skills by having to hit from the rough all the time.

Within two years, land's owner wanted to use the area for farm expansion and the club was able to get a new site of more than one hundred acres, across the CPR tracks and about a quarter mile from town. This tract also required volunteer labour so away we went again with scythes, rakes, mowers and brush cutters. We produced a splendid nine-hole layout. On many summer evenings, Marge, the girls and I packed a picnic supper and went out for nine holes, dining on the links. Dorothy started hitting long drives — and still does.

One year, my team won the Free Press Four-Man Trophy. In 1965, at the age of sixty-nine, I won the Calgary seniors' golf championship with a six-over-par seventy-seven. In 1992, at the age of ninety-six, I shot an 84 at my home Turner Valley Golf and Country Club course. That earned a brief mention in Score Magazine, Canada's leading golf publication.

When I was 74, I shot a hole-in-one. (I'll never forget the date. It was February 25, 1970.) Today, I golf at Turner Valley Golf and Country Club, where I am a proud lifetime member, every Tuesday. I get up at

6:30 a.m. and drive about sixty kilometres to the golf course. I usually golf with my buddies Jim Hampshire, Roy Haxton, Bob Pinna and Ed Shute. (We're members of Turner Valley's seniors club.) We usually golf between 8:00 a.m. and 10 a.m. Usually, I also golf on Sunday with Dorothy and Ron Pike, who are also members at Turner Valley, and friends. I use a power cart. I own it but the club lets me store it there.

While I'm playing, I often get out of the cart and walk to my next shot while whoever is riding with me takes the

PUTTING AROUND: *Golf still helps me feel healthy, whether the putts go in or come up short.*   Marianne Helm Photo

cart. It's just terrific to be able to get out on the golf course and walk around, let alone play a pretty good game of golf.

What do I get out of golf? A lot of fun, good exercise, real friendship, a lot of satisfaction and happiness. I might shoot 150 (figuratively speaking), but I'm repaid with one hundred and fifty thousand

171

laughs. My sports experience continues to motivate me. I still want to do the very best in everything I do.

Sports teach honesty and how to live and socialize with other people. They make a family very strong through group participation and loyalty. Sports make you very unselfish if you look at them properly. Not all people are talented but they can still enjoy games together. All our family participated in golf, curling, baseball, and small- game hunting. We received tremendous satisfaction. Sure, my ability to perform these activities has changed as I've gotten older, but I'm just continuing to do what I love. Not all people are talented and yet they can still enjoy activities. At any age.

Dr. Perls and Dr. Silver wrote a book, based on their study findings, entitled Living to 100, which includes some details on my life and a picture of me golfing. Living to 100 is a revelation to me. Did you know that in the United States it's estimated approximately seven thousand five hundred centenarians still live at home and look after themselves? I never knew that there were so many seniors in their later years in life. Dr. Perls and Dr. Silver are saying that there's a place in society for seniors — a very high place in their estimation. They're suggesting seniors should be recognized for their links with the past, their continued good health, and people should appreciate the work that they have done.

My life, I believe, corroborates a lot of things in there. Dr. Perls' and Dr. Silver's book tells the story of how productive seniors are to their nation and that we're becoming, more than ever, a voice that will be heard. When I was in my nineties, it was bandied about that I was a biological phenomenon. This was the city's joke but, in my opinion, I have developed a unique ability to prolong my life. I can't tell you why I've managed to live so long. I just know how I feel and what I've done to make my life successful.

Dr. Perls and Dr. Silver believe that genetics ultimately determine how long a person can live. Genetics might have played a role in my case because my maternal grandmother lived until she was one hun-

dred and four while my mother died at the age of ninety-seven and my father passed away when he was ninety-three. I believe my longevity is probably a combination of my positive attitude, faith, strong family values and relationships, and good health. By what people tell me, I'm encouraged to continue what I'm doing. I think finding a way to develop this desire is what Dr. Perls and his colleagues are after.

BIRTHDAY DANCE: I still enjoy participating in activities with young people. Chelsea Low, a student at Harold Panabaker Junior High School in Calgary was my partner at my 102nd birthday party. Chelsea played in the school band that day and stayed around to dance.
Calgary Herald Photo

As a centenarian, I have discovered that seniors can live a life of inspiration, more than anything else. You can be seen as a person of advanced age and respected for your accomplishments. I've learned a lot from that book. I've learned that I'm onto something. The joy of living. I pay the price with continued activity and the desire to continue giving people inspiration. Wherever I go, people tell me that I inspire them with my ability or my outlook on life — my positive attitude — but I don't see what the big deal is because it's just my way of life. I appreciate their words.

I'm not looking for glory but, through this book, I'm certainly looking for a way to tell people how to enjoy living — especially as seniors. I think I've accomplished that. I've got a method of living and I think

it's successful. It works for me. I take a great deal of pleasure in living. I look forward to my activities — I plan — and take joy in what I do.

I can't compare myself with Dr. Perls and Dr. Silver because they're professors and people who are recognized in life for their ability to write and to educate. I have to educate people by what I've accomplished and how I feel about my achievements, because nobody can feel any better. It's not a selfish thing at all. It's a service. The story of my longevity is something that I think I owe to all people, because I've been gifted with a long life, happiness, good family, success, and I've overcome tragedy and bereavement. My story is just the story of a person who has lived to one hundred and beyond and enjoyed a successful, happy, and productive life.

I think there's a lot of great centenarians Dr. Perls and Dr. Silver haven't uncovered. They've likely lived remarkable, but quiet, lives and are highly regarded by their own communities and their families. I hope future generations of seniors gain some inspiration from my life. All things are possible if you believe in yourself and God. I've got the attitude. I've got the desire. I have the health and determination to live out my days in a way that I am supposed to. (I think that's already determined. I don't know why but I think there is a pre-determination.)

One of my late friends, who was a wonderful guy to go fishing with, said: "Old age is hell." I never agreed with him. In my opinion, he didn't have the right attitude or want to live, probably because both he and his wife were not well.

Perhaps people who fear old age have lost the desire to live. Age doesn't frighten me. I have learned it's very important to continue your life expecting to do better. When children in the schools I visit discover that I'm over one hundred years of age, they look up in wonder.

You too can grow old gracefully. You've got to be proud of yourself and you've got to make a great effort to maintain that standard. Success will follow success. I have discovered that aging can be desirable. Aging can be fruitful. It can be an acceptance of moving into a contented life. My motivation is always there. My desire is always there.

You have to approach old age with a positive attitude, knowing that you have a place in this world and you have a purpose in life. That purpose might not be revealed to you but you may live it and inspire people.

I don't feel as if I am growing old. I just think I'm getting a little wiser each day. It's easy just to sit back in the rocking chair and enjoy what has happened, but that's not enough. You have to do more. You have to work on yourself and do what you're able to do with pleasure and enjoyment. Each little thing that you succeed in makes you stronger. I'm very thankful for the good health that I have had. I'm going to try and maintain it, stay in my own home and complete the mission that I feel I have yet to accomplish. I wanted to develop this dedication to excellence so that I might live happily. I know that I've lived quite longer than normal and I don't want to be a person that has to rely on others. I like to be individually competent.

One day, I made some crabapple jam. I'm very proud of myself because I never left a spot on the stove. That might be a little selfish but I feel very independent — and my independence means everything to me. I don't want to be excess baggage for my family. I want to make a life for myself and help others in doing the same, recalling all the good things that have happened to me in my life and the pleasure in speaking out.

What winds me up? Motivation is movement and I think you've just got to keep moving. My good health built a desire to be active. I take a great deal of happiness in motivating myself and, within my limitations, by keeping busy with things to do. I like what I do and my desire motivates me. There's something inside me that clicks to continue to do things well.

I follow a personal program. I try to plan each day to a very high level. I try to schedule something constructive every day. I write out a schedule, or itinerary, every day and strive to carry it out. (The planning actually starts the night before as I set my clothes out for the next day. I dress in the morning for what I'm going to do. I feel better getting up knowing what I'm going to put on.) I discipline myself — and

criticize myself. I have trained myself to believe in perfection. I take great pride in being able to keep up my home and cook, clean and maintain my lawns and garden.

Procrastination is bad form. I strongly avoid procrastinating because it can become a very worrisome habit. If I don't get done what I've planned to do in a given day, I'm disappointed. When I have chores to do, I start them first thing in the morning and keep after them until the afternoon. When I know there is something I have to do, and perhaps I can't do it because of bad weather, I'm ill at ease.

When I was younger, I never thought that I would be able to do these things today at my age. Even when I was preparing for retirement, I never thought that I would be able to have this kind of health or this kind of attitude and joyful, secure living. I didn't think I would be able to live this long in comfort. It can be very easy to sit down and do nothing. That's what everybody says to me: "Just sit down and enjoy yourself."

Well, that's not in me. I enjoy myself when I'm sitting down but I still accomplish things. I can't get comfortable just sitting down and doing nothing. There is something to do and I'm not going to be satisfied until I get it done. I don't have to do it in a hurry but I have to do it well. Sometimes, we have to wait until the right season to do something but, in winter, when the snow is still on the ground, I look forward to gardening and cleaning up the outside of my home, golfing, and fishing in the spring and summer. If I can't do something right away because of bad weather, I find something else to do. I might tie some flies, clean up some of my paperwork, or write letters. There are times when I have to push myself but, when the job is done, I take great satisfaction from it and relax.

This perpetual planning is a continuing feeling and it pays big rewards when I'm finished what I want to do. Such as? Satisfaction. Joy of living. I don't get down on myself but I don't let myself get into a slipshod mode. I try to keep my work at a level that I can do everything well — in time. I take a comfortable pace in everything I do. I

know the safe pace and I take it all the time. I don't rush at anything anymore — ever. I don't get sloppy about anything. Even when I'm cooking something on the stove, I'm exceptionally careful to turn off the burners afterwards. It's just a safety precaution. Two of my friends fell down the steps and they both died of injuries related to the mishaps. One of them was the vice-president of the CPR. He said: "I just took one step too many and I knew it." My other friend worked on top machinery all his life but he slipped and fell down the stairs. One lady in our club got her feet tangled in her blankets while sleeping and broke her hip. She survived but she's still disabled.

There was a time when I wasn't afraid to try anything without hurting myself, within the bounds of my strength. Now, I have to be realistic. I have reached an age where I have to be careful in everything that I do. Age takes some toll. Whatever I do, I'm more deliberate about keeping well. I still have the faith that I can do it — but I'm much more cautious. When my father was teaching me how to build things with tools that could be dangerous if not used properly, he always said: "Measure twice; cut once."

Today, I think twice before making a false move. I'm very thoughtful before I move into a danger zone. Going down the stairs, I may not need the banister but I use it. If I get up at night, I make sure that I have both feet planted on the ground before I make a move. To prevent falls, I don't climb up on chairs or ladders. I give driving very deep thought. I'm always cautious and I always obey the rules of the road.

I'm very protective of my privilege to drive. I realize I have a responsibility to be careful, not only to myself but to everybody that I encounter. Before I go out, I ask myself, Is it necessary? Is it for pleasure or necessity? Anyplace that I do go, I prepare myself for it and have a plan on how to get there. I'd never take a chance on the road. I'd rather wait for a guy to go and then go safely. I was brought up with safety in the railway. It would be a terrible thing if I got into an accident. In my view, if you lose confidence when you're behind the wheel, you better get out of the car.

I always monitor myself and feel like I have a supervisor watching me. I worked in my garden recently for seven hours one day. I took a chair out there with me. The chair demanded at least a third of the time. I'd work for about ten minutes and sit down for about five. I didn't intend to do all that work, but I did. I came out of it without a pain or an ache. I slept well that night. It's kind of a test. I was renewed that day in my yard when I worked for seven hours.

My good health built a desire to be active. This desire is in my soul. The desire is so great that I have to act upon it. When I complete the assignment that I've set for myself, I get a terrific satisfaction. I really do. I enjoy sitting down and thinking about it. During the time I'm working, I'm just as happy as I can be because I have no aches or pains. I won't be satisfied until I get the task done. It kind of takes hold of me. I know there's something to be done and I'd better do it. If it's not done, why, I'm not happy. I'm not content. I feel like it's a waste of time if I don't do something. There's only so much time. I'm happier when I'm doing something — much happier. I push myself within the bounds of reason. I like resting but I like to accomplish something every day. That's the real motivation.

I wiped all my cupboards down with Danish oil one day and cleaned all the windows. I have a plan to keep active and complete each job and I get tremendous satisfaction from doing that. After I do something I've set out to do, I enjoy complete relaxation. When I finished my work in the yard, I told myself: "Well done, Tom." I have a great deal of compassion for people who are unable to do some things — or anything — at an advanced age. Everyone needs to have a sense of accomplishment and they shouldn't forget that. They should be very proud of that accomplishment, no matter how humble it is. However, I'm realistic enough at my age to know that I have to give up some things gracefully. For instance, I probably won't be as active in curling as I have been because, sliding down the ice alongside a rock, a fall could be very painful. I have a responsibility to my family and my neighbours, who help me around my house, to maintain my health and accept assistance

when it's offered. I don't try to do too much and possibly place my health at risk.

How do I find that balance between an even keel and over-exertion? My body tells me. It doesn't respond as it ought to. The response is negative. It's quite natural. If you get in the habit of doing some things, you can slow down and do it better. How do you know when to say when? If you think about it enough before you do it, why, your mind tells you when you're ready to do it safely. How do you limit yourself and know when you can't do it? You just get tired. I don't go that far. I just don't do it until I get rested so I can do it properly. If you start something, and it isn't going anywhere, well just cease and desist and come back to it.

Again, attitude is the key. If you've got a good attitude, your whole life will change and your health will change with it — I really believe it does. How? All your movements respond to your attitude. Your body gets tuned up. You just feel that you can accomplish all that you plan to do. It's difficult to overcome physical ailments, but I have discovered that you can overcome pain with pleasant living. I take a hot bath every night and go to bed refreshed — or willing to be refreshed.

My attitude brings out my desire. All functions of my body respond. That makes work easy and very pleasant. In my opinion, you've got to keep your attitude very strong, faithful and dedicated to clean, healthy living. That means trying to stay away from drugs, alcohol. As I told you earlier, I made a pledge to my father when I was twelve years old to abstain from alcohol and tobacco. Maintaining that pledge has never been a problem. Drinking booze is not my bag. It has no appeal to me whatsoever. I get my pleasure in achievement. I heard a sermon from Dr. Schuler and he read from the Bible. He said, "If a person takes care of himself and lives a moral, clean life — free from excesses, things that are demoralizing you — you could be able to live one hundred and twenty years. It says that in the Bible. We could live to one hundred and twenty years if we have a good diet and reject all things that hurt the human body and mind."

I also think you have to have a tidy mind. I get a lot of pleasure thinking about the things I have done and I hope to do them again. It's a fulfillment and I get a great charge out of keeping my mind clear. If something is subconsciously worrying me, I track it down and get rid of it. I work hard at trying to keep myself up to date. I test myself in a lot of ways. I try to keep my memory good, my interests sharp and my body strong. You have to discipline yourself to do it too. If your mind is at rest, you can do so many things so much easier, so much better and so much faster.

If you believe everything is pleasurable, the results will come. All of my chores and responsibilities are a pleasure. Everything is just one more challenge. I record all my activities in my diary so that I can tell somebody about them and share them with others. I let my family members read my diary. If they've been away for a while, they read it and they know what I've done all the time while they were away. They're very interested in what I do and quite helpful. My diary gives them a good, comfortable feeling. They know I'm all right when they go away. I also maintain a good standard of diet — a regular diet, but not special. I have learned that you must enjoy your food. If you don't enjoy your food, you're not going to eat very much.

Following the lessons I learned from my wife, Margaret, I eat very well. She was a real good cook and, as I mentioned earlier, I follow some of her recipes now as I prepare most of my own meals. (I wasn't always that welcome in her kitchen but I knew what she was doing.) My best meal is my breakfast. I eat Quick Quaker Oats every day. (No, the company didn't pay me to give it a plug.) For lunch, I might have a boiled egg or a peanut butter sandwich and milk. At dinner time, I always make sure I eat some kind of meat — roast beef, steak, chicken or pork — and lots of potatoes, and I always have a fruit salad or a vegetable salad. I'm really fond of macaroni and cheese and sometimes mix in ground beef, but I never eat any other pasta because I don't like tomato sauce. I drink a lot of milk and water and the occasional cup of coffee. I sometimes eat dessert — pies, cakes and cookies — but I

never buy junk food like potato chips or pop.

I don't require any prescriptions on a regular basis, but I take an aspirin every day as recommended by doctors who believe it can help prevent heart problems. Occasionally, I also take a naturopathic remedy for swollen hands, which might result from arthritis. I also try to exercise every day for at least two hours. Often I combine my golf practice with exercise. I swing a golf club in my basement many times a day, hitting plastic balls into a net similar to what a football kicker uses on the sidelines to warm up. I always feel good after that. I also practice hundreds of chip shots at a park behind my home.

Sometimes I do a march from one end of the basement to the other. I do a military turn and try to emphasize a good upward stance. I ride a stationary bicycle in my basement every day or two, not to the extent that I work up a sweat but until my legs are tired. I recommend that you create a program of fitness for yourself. Do as much exercise as you can stand, an exercise that suits your capabilities. It's amazing what a little exercise like that will do. It's a wonderful feeling to get tired. If you can lay your head down to rest at night, with a clear and happy mind, you're going to really rest.

Your feelings about your physical fitness can also improve if you strive to maintain pride in your appearance by dressing well. When you dress well and you feel well, you've got the world by the tail. You become very positive. It's a delight to be in the company of the ladies at my club who dress so well. That's the way they come all the time. They feel better when they dress well — they tell me that — and I feel better when I dress well too. My trademark is my bolo tie.

Dressing well is a part of good living. It enhances your quality of living. Margaret was a marvelous dresser. She just loved clothing. The effect showed in her actions and her attitude. In my opinion, your face also reflects how you feel. You don't have to be handsome or beautiful — it's been a long time since I had hair on top of my head — but radiation from your face in conversation is delightful. My philosophy is: Greet everybody with a smile and just dwell on the good things in life.

181

You also have to exercise friendship — with people of any age. As I told you, my grandmother lived to one hundred and four and I always felt that she had outlived all of her friends. I don't feel that way about myself. My friends are young friends. They have accepted me as a good social friend and I participate in their dancing and their activities. I admire all the young people. They have a lot more privileges than we had when we were young. They encourage me by their friendliness and their desire to be involved in my life. It's embarrassing sometimes. If you respect somebody that's older and wiser than yourself, you should take encouragement from that person. Just spending a little time talking to younger people helps me. I feel that other people's interests contribute to your life and make it happier in the scheme of things.

I get great inspiration from my family and friends — every day. My mind is in the young world. I love young people. (For instance, golfer Tiger Woods is one of my sporting heroes.) I'd like younger people to know that it's very possible to be very happy in old age, but I do recognize that they have to have good help to do that — and a positive attitude.

During the taping of the documentary 100 Something, for the Discovery Channel, the show's producer Susan Papp asked me: "What keeps you so young?" Well, you know, I grow old just like anybody else but I think, possibly, the answer is that I love life. I have never put myself in a position of hurting myself or hurting my living. I've lived morally and rendered religiously. Scientific findings aside, I think it would be possible for any person to reach one hundred if they had the same positive attitude that I have. "If you could go back in time, where would you go?" Susan wondered. You know, it's funny, but I think I've reached the peak in security — enduring contentment — and that's because I have no worries.

In other words, I wouldn't want to go back to a supposedly better time in my life — because I'm at the pinnacle of my life right now. I appreciate where I've been but I've still got places to go — and things to do. My ability to survive two world wars, my wonderful wife and

family and friends, my railroad career which culminated in an executive position before retirement, and my good health have all provided me with a great life — but I'm not finished. I don't feel that I have accomplished everything. I think there are lots of areas I can improve on in making other people's lives — and my own — better.

It's easy just to sit back in the rocking chair and enjoy what has happened — but that's not enough. You have to do more, depending on what your health will allow. You have to work on yourself and do what you're able to do with pleasure and enjoyment. Each little thing that you succeed in makes you stronger. I'm very thankful for the good health that I have had. I feel that I have a mission to encourage people and make this book a success. My ultimate goal is to protect my health, stay in my own home, and maintain an extremely high quality of life for as long as possible.

No matter what might happen to my health and lifestyle in the future as I continue to get older, I know what I will always strive to do.

Carry on!

Epilogue

Now, my life has entered a different phase. The grieving and sorrowful periods have subsided, but the loss of Margaret will never leave me. My diaries tell of many lonesome days, and it took great encouragement from those close to me to get back to enjoying every day life. I elected to stay in my home and take care of it, to plant my gardens and cook my meals. Marge's illness was a little preparation for this. I have improved, and even enjoy, my kitchen activities. I treat myself well, eat good food, stay active and see friends and family.

I have wonderful health, bestowed upon me by God and, I am certain, by the good care of my dear wife all through our married life. I do miss her terribly, and try to do the things she would have me do. I have little conversations with her — she is very close. My good health allows me to travel and enjoy it.

As I mentioned at the beginning of this book, I am still able to drive my car with an unrestricted license and this has brought the attention from the media. The trips to New York and California, and the other interviews, were exciting times, but I like the routine of life at home. There is always so much to do. I keep a schedule, I rise early, and get to my work. On Sundays, I take much comfort from Dr. Schuller, host of television's Hour of Power. He gives me great inspiration. On that day too, I call Joyce or she calls me and, almost always, I go to Dorothy's for dinner. That is a very good day.

I also have many visitors. My brother Wallace comes from Winnipeg to visit regularly. He, too, is in good health, except for an imbalance with which he deals admirably. We have become close friends again after focusing for many years on our families and careers. We experience the greatest pleasure in talking over old times — and current times. My wife's sister Jean Norvell of Vancouver, whom I mentioned

earlier, comes to be with me frequently and she is of great comfort to me. Jean is a lovely lady, a great companion, and adds a dimension to the home and the meals. My sister's daughter, Joan, and her husband, Don, come from Regina for golf and fishing which I'm always willing to do. Joan's daughter, Anne, who is an outdoor tour guide keeps in close touch with me and is a cheerful, bright, presence.

I must sing a little paean of praise to my neighbours on both sides, who are extremely caring and watchful of me. Bruce and Matil Spies and their three fine children — Katherine, Lisa and Adam — extend friendship and a helping hand on so many occasions. They go about this so quietly, without fanfare. Suddenly, my walks are free from snow or I have a warm dish for supper.

Ron and Mary Ede, formerly on my other side but now living in Canmore, Alberta, have also been so very kind. We will never forget Mary for all the times she ran over to be with Marge when she was ill, bringing some fresh baked treat and, always, some cheering conversation. This street is probably like many streets all over North America, but it does seem to have a greater number of concerned and caring people who make the word "neighbour" become synonymous with "caring friend."

Vince Thormin, a retired minister, visits me regularly and we share much, as he has lost his wife of many years and brings his inspiration to our conversation.

I still golf in summer. In deepest winter, in my basement recreation room, I ride my stationary bike, drive a plastic golf ball into a sheet, tie flies and dream of waters to explore. When the season opens, I go fishing whenever I have a companion. I write letters, many letters, often to Joyce, my grandchildren and dear friends. I am also faithful to my diaries.

Life is still rich beyond expectation. I draw on the great faith inspired by my parents. In times of great distress, I "take it to the Lord" in prayer and he frees me from my burdens and restores my soul. I think of all those good friends and dear family who are gone now. They

pass before my eyes and are not forgotten, especially my wife, whose presence will forever pervade my home. My children and my grand-children are the touchstone, the objects of my love and caring. This, then is my story, my song saying to you that the wonders and beauties of life never leave me. It continues to be a time of discovery.

My parting advice? Do not be afraid — of anything.

OUT TAKES

IN THE PICTURE: My grand-daughters Margaret, left, and Nancy, right, surround their dad, Ron Pike while my daughter Dorothy sits beside me.

FUN IN SUN: My daughter Joyce Aoyagi, enjoys a visit with her grandchildren (two of my great-grandchildren) Nathan Worthington and Kate Wood at her home in Los Altos, California.

Index

About the Co-author

Monte Stewart joined the Calgary Herald in October, 1987. He covers seniors' affairs and a wide variety of issues including crime, politics, education and health. He has also covered sports, including the Calgary Flames and the rest of the National Hockey League. The Vancouver native has also served as Sports Editor at the Prince Rupert Daily News (1985-86) and sports reporter with the Grande Prairie Daily-Herald Tribune (1986-87). His freelance articles have also appeared in such publications as the Toronto Star, Profit Magazine, and San Jose Mercury-News. Stewart, who is single, resides in northwest Calgary. This is his first book.

To Order More Copies of
CARRY ON

Telephone Orders: Please call (403) 256-2754

On-line Orders: Please visit Tom Spear's website at **www.tomspear.com**

Postal Orders: Please complete the following —

Yes, I would like to purchase more copies of *Carry On: Reaching Beyond 100*! Please send me ___ copies of *Carry On* for $24.95 plus $4.00 shipping and handling for the first copy and $2.00 shipping and handling for each additional copy.

NAME _____

ADDRESS _____

_____

CITY _____

PROV./STATE _____

POSTAL CODE _____

I have enclosed a cheque or money order for _____

Mail To:

Falcon Press
12 Shawinigan Way S.W.
Calgary, Alberta
T2Y 2A1

Please allow four to six weeks for delivery.

Notes

Notes

About Tom Spear

Tom Spear was born Oct. 22, 1896 in Galt, Ont. The second eldest of four children, he grew up in rural Manitoba as his father David Spear, a Presbyterian minister and mother, Margaret Ballingal Spear, moved around the province to serve their congregations.

Outside of war duty, Mr. Spear never missed a day's work in fifty years of service with the Canadian Pacific Railway between 1912-1963. He also enjoyed seventy years of marriage with Margaret Bell Hooper Spear, who died March 28, 1992.

Mr. Spear is also a veteran of both world wars. In World War I, he served as a wireless communications operator in England, France and Germany. During World War II, he enlisted with the Royal Canadian Air Force and rose to the rank of acting wing commander while serving exclusively in Canada.

He has also played a prominent role in community affairs, wherever he has lived. He was a member of the British Empire Service League (forerunner of the Royal Canadian Legion) and earned election as a school board trustee and town councillor in Emerson, Manitoba in the 1920s and 1930s. He has also served as an executive of golf, hockey and curling clubs in Emerson and Calgary and held executive positions within the United Church.

He was nominated for the Order of the British Empire (equivalent to the Order of Canada) three times and, in recent years, has received several awards. In November, 1998, he was named a Knight in the French Legion of Honour because of his World War I service and received the Liberation of Belgium Medal. Mr. Spear is also a recipient of the prestigious Rotary Club Paul Harris Fellow for Community Service.

Mr. Spear and his brother Wallace of Winnipeg are also participants in a Harvard University study on centenarian siblings, designed to help explain the causes of diseases, like arthritis, which strike the elderly.

Tom Spear currently lives in Calgary, Alberta, Canada.

CANADIAN CATALOGUING IN PUBLICATION DATA

Spear, Tom, 1896-

Carry on: reaching beyond 100

Includes Index.

ISBN 0-9685465-0-1

1. Spear, Tom, 1896- 2. Centenarians—Alberta— Biography. 3. Alberta— Biography. I. Stewart, Monte, 1962- II. Title.

HE2808.2.S64A3 1999 971.23'02'092 C99-900727-0

Cover design by Renee Coulman
Front and back cover photos by Marianne Helm
Falcon Press logo design by Bruce Full
Edited by David Bly & Duane Beazer
Printed and bound in Canada

Published by
Falcon Press
12 Shawinigan Way S.W.
Calgary, Alberta, Canada
T2Y 2A1

Carry On
Reaching Beyond 100

An Autobiography By Tom Spear
with Monte Stewart

Published By Falcon Press, Calgary, Alberta